KT-468-358

# Contents

Introduction ...................................................... 5

Chapter **1** Food for a Healthy Heart ............................... 7

Chapter **2** Food for Better Bones ................................. 25

Chapter **3** Sweet But Deadly ..................................... 47

Chapter **4** Food for Thought ..................................... 65

Chapter **5** Healthy Tums ......................................... 89

Chapter **6** A Diet for Great Skin ................................ 107

Chapter **7** Therapeutic Eating Plans ............................. 127

Chapter **8** Recipes .............................................. 145

Help List ......................................................... 155

Book List ......................................................... 163

References ........................................................ 165

Glossary .......................................................... 167

6840402826 1 648

# FOOD FOR HEALTH

## The Essential Guide

**Need — 2 — Know**

Sara
Kirkham

**LEICESTER LIBRARIES**

| | |
|---|---|
| **Askews** | 03-Nov-2010 |
| | £9.99 |
| | |

First published in Great Britain in 2010 by
**Need2Know**
Remus House
Coltsfoot Drive
Peterborough
PE2 9JX
Telephone 01733 898103
Fax 01733 313524
www.need2knowbooks.co.uk

Need2Know is an imprint of Forward Press Ltd.
www.forwardpress.co.uk
All Rights Reserved
© Sara Kirkham 2010
SB ISBN 978-1-86144-095-2
Cover photograph: istockphoto

# Introduction

What could be better than finding an easy, inexpensive and healthy way to make you feel and look the picture of health? The answer you are looking for is right in front of you, in the foods that you eat every day.

*Food for Health – The Essential Guide* is the ultimate nutritional guide to self sufficient health and wellbeing. It will provide you with the tools to maximise your health or improve specific conditions using everyday foods. While eating an optimum nutrition diet will have the greatest effect upon your health, there's no need for an all or nothing approach, and this book provides a range of options: from making simple dietary changes right through to following an optimum nutrition eating plan. Whether you want to reduce the risk of hereditary conditions such as arthritis or diabetes, improve existing health conditions such as high cholesterol, or follow a diet to reduce inflammation, this book provides the know how.

Doctors and healthcare professionals may provide some guidance on how to adapt your diet to improve conditions such as indigestion or diabetes, but the science of nutrition and how food affects our body is a specialist subject, so you are assured of the best advice from a qualified nutritionist or dietitian.

You may be referred to a state registered dietitian by your GP, but a full consultation with a nutritionist or freelance dietitian is still helpful. Details of how to find a qualified practitioner in your area are included in the help list. Prices for a consultation vary, but expect to pay approximately £40-50 per hour, which usually includes dietary guidelines and an eating plan to follow. Follow-up appointments usually cost less and the number of appointments required varies from a single consultation to appointments spanning several months.

However, if you want to take greater control of your own health and learn how to be your own 'food doctor', this is the book for you. *Food for Health – The Essential Guide* opens the door to a healthier way of life for you and your family through simple dietary changes all supported by research. There is also a helpful glossary at the end to explain the terms used throughout the book.

'If the doctors of today don't become nutritionists, the nutritionists will become the doctors of tomorrow.'

In each chapter you will find:

- A simple explanation of what each condition is.

- A list of superfoods to help improve the condition or ease its symptoms.

- Scientific research to support the dietary recommendations.

- Simple tips to help you make dietary changes – how to fit recommended foods into your diet, ways to maximise nutrient content and meal ideas.

- Information on therapeutic supplements, herbs and spices.

Recipes and seven-day eating plans for various disease conditions are included in chapters 7 and 8.

Whether you're ready to give your diet a complete overhaul or you're just looking for quick and easy ways to eat a healthier diet, you can choose a way of changing your diet that suits you:

'Let food be
your medicine,
and medicine
be your food.'

Hippocrates AD390.

- Quick changes – watch out for tick lists to show you how to fit more of a specific food into your diet.

- Ready for a bit more – aim to make more than one dietary change, and try the recipes as well.

- Diet overhaul – follow one of the seven-day eating plans.

*Food for Health – The Essential Guide* offers the ultimate guide to improving your health through diet – handed to you 'on a plate'! All you have to do is eat it!

# Chapter One

# Food for a Healthy Heart

Coronary heart disease, or cardiovascular disease, is one of the most common causes of death, causing 29.2% of global deaths according to a World Health Report in 2003. Despite public health campaigns to reduce cholesterol and increase activity levels, most people still haven't made the lifestyle changes required to reduce the risk of heart disease. Yet there are several simple dietary changes that can significantly improve the health of your heart, postponing or even reducing the onset of heart disease.

## What is heart disease?

Heart disease is usually a combination of high blood pressure, atherosclerosis ('furring up' of the arteries) and high cholesterol levels, although other factors are involved. Although we commonly use the term 'heart disease', these conditions also affect the blood vessels going to and from the heart because substances such as fats are carried in the bloodstream.

### Hypertension

Hypertension is continued high blood pressure. A 'normal' blood pressure reading is 120/80, where the first figure is systolic blood pressure (when the heart is contracting) and the second figure is diastolic blood pressure (when the heart is filling with blood). This figure tends to increase from our mid-twenties as we age. The higher the blood pressure, the greater the likelihood of damage to the inside of the artery walls. Once damaged, fatty substances are more likely to stick to the inside of these blood vessels and 'fur up' the arteries, causing atherosclerosis.

## Atherosclerosis

Atherosclerosis is the result of the 'furring up' on the inside of the artery walls. As this plaque formation builds up, it reduces the space for blood to travel through, which increases blood pressure, creating even more damage to the artery walls. Once the smooth inner membrane of an artery is damaged, fatty substances are more likely to stick to its rough surface, worsening the atherosclerosis and narrowing the artery even more. Although high blood pressure and atherosclerosis are two separate conditions, they each cause the other.

Normal artery

Fatty plaque build up
in artery wall

## Arteriosclerosis

This is a hardening of the artery walls often found alongside atherosclerosis. Our artery walls are made of the foods that we eat, the types of fats we consume and the balance of minerals like calcium, magnesium, sodium and potassium. This all affects how flexible our artery walls are. Eating too many 'bad' fats (also known as hydrogenated, saturated, refined or trans fats) creates rigid artery walls, whereas 'good' fats (also known as polyunsaturated fats) from fish, nuts and seeds promote flexibility. A diet high in salt (sodium) or calcium, or not enough magnesium, also contributes to rigid artery walls which fail to 'give' when blood pressure increases, making them more likely to be damaged. Smoking also contributes to arteriosclerosis.

## Cholesterol

Not all cholesterol is bad for us; only oxidised low density lipoprotein (LDL) cholesterol ('bad' cholesterol) increases the risk of heart disease. Our diet only provides approximately 20% of our cholesterol. We make the rest ourselves, using it to form cell membranes, to make hormones and to form bile for fat digestion. High levels of high density lipoprotein (HDL) cholesterol ('good' cholesterol) helps to counteract high levels of 'bad' cholesterol.

Reducing cholesterol in your diet has little effect on your cholesterol levels, so what can you do if you have high cholesterol?

- 'Bad' fats seem to increase production of cholesterol in the liver, so cut down on fatty meats, full-fat dairy produce, cakes, biscuits and ice cream.
- Reduce any excess body fat around your middle (central obesity), as this increases the amount of 'bad' cholesterol in the liver.

## Oxidation

Oxidation occurs naturally throughout the body, but without enough antioxidants such as vitamin C or E to keep it in check, oxidation can become a problem. Oxidation occurs when an unstable atom or molecule, also known as a free radical, attaches to molecules or cells and destabilises the molecule or cell next to it. This can result in a chain reaction of molecular damage causing cell damage, mutations or cell death. Heated and processed fats (trans and hydrogenated fats) are the most likely to become oxidised.

When LDL cholesterol or refined fats become oxidised, they are more likely to damage artery walls, and in trying to repair this damage, a build up of blood cells and fibres create plaque. This then contributes to atherosclerosis; the deposits inside the arteries made from different types of blood cells, calcium and the 'bad' cholesterol begin to block the inside of the artery where blood flows through, contributing to heart disease.

So, it seems that several factors contribute to heart disease:

- Increased blood pressure.
- Too much 'bad' fat in the diet.

'Patients with normal cholesterol levels have the same death rate as those with high cholesterol, suggesting that cholesterol only plays a partial role in heart disease.'

▓ Oxidation of fats.

▓ Stored body fat around the middle.

# What does a heart-healthy diet look like?

There are a number of ways that your diet can help protect you against heart disease:

▓ You can reduce your overall fat, sugar and calorie intake to reduce the risk of central obesity.

▓ You can reduce the amount of fats that you eat, particularly refined fats and cholesterol, as these are most likely to become oxidised.

▓ You can eat foods that will help you to build healthy artery walls.

▓ You can eat more antioxidants to limit oxidation.

▓ You can eat foods that increase 'good' cholesterol and reduce 'bad' cholesterol levels.

▓ You can reduce the amount of salt in your diet, which will reduce the risk of high blood pressure.

## Limit sugars and refined carbohydrate foods

There is a connection between fat stored around the middle, poor blood sugar regulation and high blood pressure; having all three is a condition called metabolic syndrome or syndrome X, and this increases your risk of heart disease and Type 2 diabetes. Too much sugar in the diet contributes to weight gain and can also increase cholesterol oxidation.

The excess sugar from too many cakes, pastries, sweets, chocolate and white bread (refined carbohydrates) causes insulin resistance and high blood sugar (see chapter 3 for more information). Obesity and insulin resistance are both powerful risk factors for heart disease, and fat around the middle secretes inflammatory substances, similar to hormones, which can increase blood pressure and cholesterol levels.

# Are you at risk?

Knowing your waist circumference or waist-hip ratio can help you to discover whether you are storing excess fat around the middle.

## Waist circumference

Waist circumferences of over 88cm for women and over 102cm for men increase the risk of Type 2 diabetes and heart disease. Here are the recommended guidelines suggested by the NHS.

| Waist circumference guidelines for women | Waist circumference guidelines for men |
|---|---|
| Ideal: less than 80cm (32in). | Ideal: less than 94cm (37in). |
| High: 80cm to 88cm (32 to 35in). | High: 94cm to 102cm (37 to 40in). |
| Very high: more than 88cm (35in). | Very high: more than 102cm (40in). |

The Ashwell® shape chart overleaf illustrates how your waist measurement might be affecting your health.

## Waist-hip ratio

Your waist-hip ratio compares the circumference of your waist to your hips – the more 'apple' shaped you are, the higher the health risks.

| Women | Men |
|---|---|
| Ideal: less than 0.8. | Ideal: less than 0.9. |
| Too high: 0.85 or more. | Too high: 1 or more. |

'Being "pear" shaped rather than "apple" shaped may actively protect against diabetes and heart disease.'

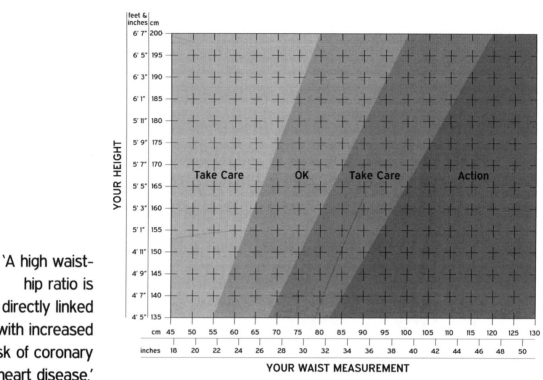

© Dr Margaret Ashwell.

'A high waist-hip ratio is directly linked with increased risk of coronary heart disease.'

## How to calculate your waist-hip ratio

To calculate your waist-hip ratio, simply divide your waist measurement by your hip measurement.

$$\frac{\text{Waist } 80}{\text{Hips } 110} = 0.72$$

Make sure that both measurements are either in inches or in centimetres. To calculate your waist-hip ratio online, go to www.besthealth.com/besthealth/wellness/waisthip.htm.

Need2Know

# Eat the right types of fats

Not all fats are bad. Saturated and trans fats (found in many bakery and processed foods) have been linked with heart disease, whereas polyunsaturated fats, such as those found in fish and nuts, and monounsaturated fats, found in olive oil or avocado, are linked with a reduced risk of heart disease.

'Bad' fats make your cells rigid, therefore reducing the flexibility of artery walls and making them more at risk of damage. These fats also attach to the plaques inside artery walls, contributing to atherosclerosis. In comparison, the 'good' fats found in fish, vegetable oils, nuts and seeds help to form more flexible artery walls.

Higher fish consumption as part of a Mediterranean diet has been linked with lower cholesterol and fewer fats in the blood. Fresh or frozen fish is the best option, and there are more essential fatty acids known to promote heart health in oily fish than non-oily fish.

Eat more fish by:

- Swapping a breakfast fry-up for kippers.
- Enjoying kedgeree or sardines on toast for brunch or lunch.
- Adding salmon or tuna to sandwiches instead of cheese, egg or meat.
- Swapping meat for fish in at least two evening meals per week.

White fish, such as cod or haddock, do contain heart-healthy fats, but as they store more fat in their liver than in their flesh, you consume fewer of these fats when you eat non-oily fish. Although oily fish store fat in their flesh, the 'good' fats are mostly lost during the canning process, so tinned fish will contain lower levels of 'good' fats, similar to the levels found in non-oily fish.

'The UK Food Standards Agency (FSA) recommends that we eat two to four portions of fish a week, of which one to two portions should be oily fish.'

## Reducing 'bad' fat

Swapping meat for fish is one way to decrease your intake of saturated 'bad' fats and increase polunsaturated 'good' fats. Decreasing full-fat dairy produce and limiting egg consumption is another way to decrease 'bad' fat intake.

- Enjoy a peppered mackerel or walnut Waldorf salad rather than an egg or cheese salad.

- Have hummus or tahini instead of creamy dips or mayonnaise.

- Add mackerel, salmon or tuna to salads instead of cheese or egg.

- Go vegetarian for some meals, replacing animal produce with beans and pulses.

## Olive oil – cardio-protective properties

The Mediterranean-style diet has been repeatedly linked with a decreased risk of heart disease due to reduced cholesterol and blood pressure measurements, improved blood sugar regulation and reduced damage and inflammation in artery walls. Plant foods and oils such as avocados, nuts, seeds and olive oil are rich in healthy monounsaturated fats.

Add heart-healthy fats to your diet by:

- Dipping your bread in olive oil rather than spreading butter on it.

- Adding avocado or vegetable oil dressings to salads rather than cheese, egg or meats.

- Cooking with olive oil.

- Snacking on nuts and seeds rather than biscuits and cakes.

Making all of these changes will drastically reduce your intake of 'bad' fats and dietary cholesterol.

# Fruits and vegetables

Fruits and vegetables offer several benefits in a heart-healthy diet:

- Many of these foods are rich in antioxidants, helping to reduce oxidation.

- They are lower in calories and fats, reducing central obesity and Type 2 diabetes.

- Many fruits and vegetables are rich in potassium and naturally low in salt, and can help to maintain a healthy blood pressure.

- Fruits and vegetables contain types of fibre known to help lower cholesterol levels.

## Antioxidants

Oxidation is a serious contributor to heart disease. However, it can be reduced by nutrients called antioxidants, and several large-scale studies have illustrated eating a lot of antioxidants benefits the health of your arteries. Some plant nutrients (also known as phytonutrients) have been found to have a powerful antioxidant effect.

For example, tomatoes contain a nutrient called lycopene which has been found to have several cardio-protective properties:

- It has a high antioxidant content.
- It regulates cholesterol production.
- It stimulates the break down of 'bad' cholesterol.
- Low blood levels of lycopene have been linked with a higher incidence of death from heart disease.

## Fruit and vegetables can reduce blood pressure

Many large population studies show a positive association between fruit and vegetable consumption and decreased risk of heart disease. One of the ways that fruit and vegetables can help to reduce the risk of heart disease is by lowering blood pressure.

## Fruits and vegetables reduce cholesterol

Regular consumption of fruit and vegetables can help to reduce your risk of heart disease by lowering cholesterol levels. Apple and garlic are repeatedly said to give good cholesterol-lowering results, as are other foods like chicory and asparagus. It is the fibre in these foods that is the active ingredient responsible for the cholesterol lowering benefits.

The cholesterol in our bloodstream comes from two sources – cholesterol that we eat (dietary cholesterol) and the cholesterol that our liver makes. The chemical compounds found in plant fibre compete with cholesterol for absorption in the digestive tract, blocking the amount of dietary cholesterol that can be absorbed. Cholesterol is carried in bile from the liver and squirted from the gall bladder into the first section of the small intestine, the duodenum, during food digestion. Although most of the cholesterol is reabsorbed into the body and recycled, fibre absorbs some of it, carrying it out of the body in the faeces.

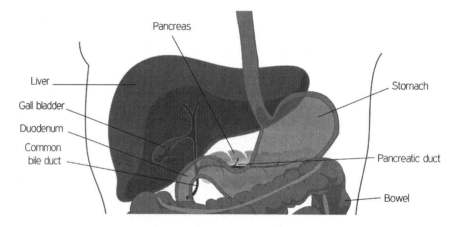

Many fruits and vegetables contain fibre which will help to lower cholesterol, but inulin is a type of fibre which is really effective at carrying cholesterol out of the body. Inulin is found in foods such as garlic, onion, asparagus, Jerusalem artichoke and chicory. The fibre in oats is also very effective at reducing cholesterol levels.

## Plant sterol-enhanced foods

Plant sterols and stanols (phytosterols) are natural plant nutrients added to foods such as margarines, yoghurts and soft cheeses to reduce cholesterol. These nutrients have been proven to lower overall and 'bad' cholesterol, but better results have been obtained by combining foods enriched with these nutrients with a healthier overall diet.

| Reduction in cholesterol from using nutrient-enriched foods | Reduction in cholesterol from using nutrient-enriched foods plus a healthier diet |
|---|---|
| Total cholesterol ↓ 10% | Total cholesterol ↓ 22.34% |
| Bad cholesterol ↓ 14% | Bad cholesterol ↓ 29.71% |

(Source: Buckley *et al.*, 2007.)

Studies have shown that phytosterols added to foods are most helpful in reducing existing high cholesterol levels rather than preventing high cholesterol levels from developing. However, a diet rich in fruits and vegetables will help to reduce the development of high cholesterol levels which may then contribute to heart disease.

Although phytosterols can lower cholesterol, they can also have the unwanted effect of reducing carotenoid levels. Carotenoids are antioxidants that fight cell damage and support immune function, so it is important not to upset the level of one nutrient by over-consuming another. Eating foods rich in carotenoids will help to provide plenty of this important antioxidant.

Carotenoid-rich foods include:

- Carrots.
- Sweet potato.
- Squash and pumpkin.
- Peaches and apricots.

Including phytosterol-enriched foods in your diet will be even more effective at reducing cholesterol if you also make the following changes to your diet:

- Decrease your intake of 'bad' fats by eating less full-fat dairy foods, eggs, meats and bakery products like biscuits and cakes.
- Swap butter for a spread enriched with phytosterols.
- Swap full-fat yoghurts for lower fat, phytosterol-enriched yoghurts or soya yoghurts.
- Choose low-fat milk enriched with phytosterols.

'For a healthy-heart diet, eat porridge made with soya milk and added fruit for breakfast, a large salad with chicory, onion and asparagus at lunchtime, and fish with broccoli and garlic-roasted squash and carrots for dinner.'

- Eat plenty of high-fibre fruit, vegetables, oats and beans, which also help to reduce the amount of circulating cholesterol in the body.

## Garlic – cardiovascular superfood

Both onion and garlic were used in ancient Egypt, Greece and Italy for heart disease. Garlic contains a number of sulphur compounds which give it its strong smell but are also extremely beneficial for our health. In addition to immune-supportive, anti-tumour and anti-carcinogenic benefits, garlic has several properties beneficial to the cardiovascular system:

- It 'thins' the blood, making it less likely to clot.
- It reduces blood pressure by widening blood vessels.
- It reduces fats in the blood.
- It contains inulin fibre which helps to reduce 'bad' cholesterol.

For allicin, one of the main therapeutic compounds in garlic, to be most active, the garlic should be crushed, left for up to 10 minutes and then eaten raw. Crushing, slicing or pressing garlic activates the enzyme that forms the active compounds that have heart-healthy properties. Some of these compounds are still viable with up to six minutes of boiling or oven roasting, so garlic still retains some therapeutic properties with light cooking if it is crushed.

To enjoy the heart-healthy benefits of garlic:

- Eat crushed, sliced or grated raw garlic.
- Crush, slice, grate or press the garlic and leave for up to 10 minutes to get the maximum goodness.
- Cook garlic moderately for no more than six minutes.

Although garlic capsules are less pungent, their effectiveness is dependent upon how the garlic capsules are manufactured. If the active ingredients from garlic are concentrated in high enough amounts and remain active in the garlic capsule, cardiovascular benefits have been recorded (Sobenin *et al.*, 2009).

# Red wine

Data from Europe, North America, Asia and Australia shows fewer instances of heart disease amongst those that consume a moderate amount of alcohol, in comparison with non-drinkers or heavy drinkers. France and other Mediterranean countries have lower levels of cardiovascular disease, despite the same risk factors for diabetes, high blood pressure and high cholesterol.

It seems that if a person drinks a moderate amount of alcohol, particularly red wine, there may still be damaged arteries and increased blood pressure caused by other lifestyle factors, but this damage is somehow offset by the relaxation in the artery walls and less blood clotting. This appears to be due to consumption of one to two glasses of red wine daily, and is partly due to the nutrients in the grapes used to make the wine. These nutrients appear to have a relaxing effect upon the artery walls, making them less liable to damage from elevated blood pressure.

## Why is red wine a heart-healthy drink?

- The alcohol and plant nutrients found in red wine both exert a relaxing effect upon the artery walls. This allows the artery to expand to accommodate higher blood flow or higher blood pressure, preventing damage to the artery wall that might create atherosclerosis.

- Drinking one to two glasses of red wine daily can increase your 'good' cholesterol by approximately 12%. The 'good' cholesterol reduces the amount of 'bad' cholesterol in the bloodstream and limits the risk of atherosclerosis. In addition to this, the antioxidants in red wine limit the oxidation of 'bad' cholesterol, further reducing fatty cholesterol deposits.

- Lastly, the nutrients in red wine have an anti-inflammatory effect and limit clot formation.

However, although a small amount of alcohol may reduce the risk of heart disease, consuming too much is detrimental to good health. But if you do drink, it seems a good idea to limit consumption to one to two drinks daily, have a few days alcohol-free each week and drink red wine as your chosen tipple!

# Things to reduce for a healthy heart

## The effects of caffeine

Caffeine, found in coffee, tea, some fizzy drinks and chocolate, makes our body produce the hormone adrenaline. One of the effects of adrenaline is that it increases blood pressure by temporarily narrowing the small arteries in the body. It is this increase in blood pressure that results in the kidneys producing more urine in an attempt to lower blood pressure by getting rid of some of the water, which is why drinking tea and coffee increases the frequency of visits to the toilet!

Adrenaline increases the amount of sugar and fats in the bloodstream for energy – but think what you are usually doing when drinking a cup of coffee; it's not usually using up this extra energy by exercising! Circulating fatty acids without a job to do increases the risk of them sticking to the inside of arterial walls, worsening any existing build up of fatty deposits, which in turn can increase blood pressure further.

However, it is still unclear how consistent increase of blood pressure from drinking caffeine affects long-term cardiovascular health, particularly if high blood pressure or atherosclerosis already exists. Although drinking coffee increases blood pressure (Buscemi *et al.*, 2010), Mineharu *et al.* found that total caffeine intake from drinking coffee, green tea or oolong tea is associated with a reduced risk of death from heart disease. It seems like the jury is still out on this one!

## Ways to reduce caffeine intake

Limit your caffeine intake to no more than three cups of caffeinated drinks each day, and try to reduce your intake by:

- Drinking alternatives such as herbal teas, or coffee alternatives such as Barleycup.
- Reducing the number of drinks of tea, coffee or cola you drink daily.
- Making tea or coffee weaker.

Need2Know

- Swapping large mugs for cups and using small glasses for cola or other drinks containing caffeine.

- Not missing meals, as a low blood sugar level prompts you to drink caffeinated drinks.

# A word about salt

High salt (sodium chloride) consumption has been linked with elevated blood pressure, and a diet low in salt and high in fruit and vegetables has been proven to significantly reduce blood pressure. Fruit and vegetables are naturally low in sodium but often rich in potassium, a mineral which helps to counteract the effects of sodium in the body.

## Ways to reduce salt intake

- Stop adding salt to cooking.

- Don't add salt to your food.

- Check food labels for high salt or sodium content.

- Avoid high salt foods such as Marmite, anchovies, salted crisps and nuts.

- Watch out for high salt foods that don't necessarily taste salty, such as cheese, bread and pizza.

- Eat plenty of potassium-rich foods to counteract the effects of salt – fill up on fruit, vegetables and juices.

The Food Standards Agency currently recommends limiting your salt intake to 6g daily. However, food labels may show the content as 'sodium' or 'salt', because it is the sodium part of sodium chloride which affects our blood pressure rather than the chloride part. If a food label only shows the sodium content, you have to calculate the amount of salt in it by multiplying the sodium content by 2.5. For example, if a portion of food contains 0.8g of sodium, it will contain about 2g of salt.

'Start checking the salt content on tinned and packaged foods and choose low salt products. A high salt food contains more than 1.5g of salt per 100g (or 0.6g sodium per 100g), and a low salt food contains 0.3g salt or less per 100g (or 0.1g sodium).'

# Supplements to help

## Vitamin C

Vitamin C may reduce heart disease by protecting 'bad' cholesterol from oxidation and reducing 'bad' cholesterol levels.

Boost your vitamin C intake by:

- Snacking on citrus fruits and kiwis.
- Adding berries to breakfast cereals, yoghurts and desserts.
- Munching on raw peppers in salads, sandwiches and with dips.
- Adding dark green leafy vegetables to salads, sandwiches and dinners.

## Vitamin E

Vitamin E has several benefits, largely due to its antioxidant properties which help to prevent cholesterol becoming oxidised and causing atherosclerosis, thrombosis, stroke and heart attacks. Vitamin E protects 'bad' cholesterol from oxidative damage and can reduce the rate of heart attacks in those with existing heart disease.

Boost your vitamin E intake by:

- Snacking on nuts and seeds, especially Brazil nuts, almonds and hazelnuts.
- Drizzling high quality, cold vegetable oils onto salads.
- Adding pine nuts or sunflower seeds to salads and stir-fries.
- Adding wheat germ to cereals or yoghurts.
- Adding avocado to salad sandwiches, salads and wraps.

Vitamin E works in conjunction with vitamin C – the effects of each vitamin are increased by the other, so a heart healthy diet should be rich in both of these antioxidants.

While including foods rich in these nutrients will certainly benefit your health, high doses of vitamins may be necessary for you to benefit from some of these therapeutic effects. It is recommended that you consult a qualified nutritional practitioner for a safe and effective dietary and supplement prescription.

# Summing Up

To reduce the risk of heart disease:

- Limit your consumption of sugars and refined carbohydrate foods such as cakes.
- Eat less saturated and refined fats.
- Don't eat too much fat overall and keep body fat levels low.
- Eat plenty of oily fish which provides healthy polyunsaturated fats.
- Use olive oil or vegetable oils rather than saturated fats like butter.
- Eat at least five servings of low sodium, potassium-rich fruit and vegetables a day.
- Eat soya products, beans, oats and inulin-rich asparagus, Jerusalem artichoke and chicory to help reduce circulating cholesterol.
- Eat two cloves of garlic daily.
- If you do drink alcohol, limit your intake to one unit a day and consider swapping to red wine.
- Limit caffeine consumption.
- Reduce salt intake.
- Boost your vitamin A and E levels.

| Stick to... | Stay away from... |
| --- | --- |
| Fish. | Saturated or refined fats. |
| Garlic. | Refined carbohydrates. |
| Red wine. | Too much alcohol. |
| Fruit and vegetables. | Salt. |
| Oats, beans and inulin-rich vegetables. | Caffeine. |
| Olive oil. | |
| Nuts and seeds. | |
| Soya foods. | |

# Chapter Two

# Food for Better Bones

Over 80% of us will suffer with degenerative joint disease in our lifetime – approximately 400,000 people in the UK have rheumatoid arthritis and 80-85% of people over 70 have osteoarthritis. The number of arthritis sufferers is increasing: people are living longer and therefore are more likely to experience osteoarthritis, and being overweight (also on the increase) exacerbates both of these conditions. However, there are a number of other dietary factors that can either contribute to, or reduce the risk of, bone and joint complaints.

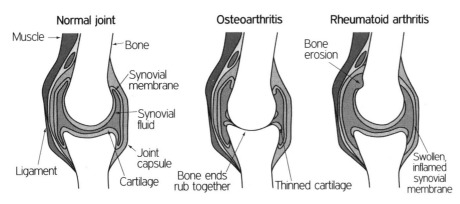

## Rheumatoid arthritis

Rheumatoid arthritis is an inflammatory autoimmune condition. Autoimmune conditions occur when your immune system, which usually fights infection, attacks part of the body. In rheumatoid arthritis, the lining of your joints is attacked, causing them to become inflamed, swollen and painful. Initially, the joints of the hands and feet are affected, but any joint may become affected. At present there is no known cure for rheumatoid arthritis, but symptoms can be eased and the progression of the condition can be slowed down.

Rheumatoid arthritis develops when immune cells infiltrate the joint fluid and begin to attack the bone and cartilage. As the bone becomes eroded, cysts form and osteoporosis may also occur. Joint fluid, which normally enables easy movement, is displaced by functionless tissue, followed by inflammation and cartilage erosion. Separate bones may even fuse together.

The risk factors for rheumatoid arthritis can include:

- Your gender – women are up to three times more likely to develop rheumatoid arthritis than men.

- Your age – it occurs most commonly between the ages of 30 and 50 (average age at diagnosis is 28), but it can occur in older people and in children.

- Your family history – rheumatoid arthritis in your family increases your risk because certain genes are thought to make some people more susceptible to developing the disease.

- Whether you smoke – smoking depletes the body of essential antioxidants that could otherwise support immune function and help to counteract inflammation.

Although you can't change your age, gender or family history, you can reduce your risk of getting rheumatoid arthritis by not smoking, and you can make dietary changes which may reduce your risk or ease existing symptoms.

## Dietary factors to help combat rheumatoid arthritis

To help fight the risk and symptoms of rheumatoid arthritis, your diet needs to be focused on foods that will improve your immune function. The main points to remember are:

- Boost your immune function to reduce the risk of infection (and therefore reduce your risk of developing rheumatoid arthritis).

- Omit or reduce foods that aggravate your symptoms.

- Eat foods with anti-inflammatory properties to help reduce the inflammation.

Autoimmune conditions such as rheumatoid arthritis often occur after infection, so eating plenty of antioxidant-rich foods to boost your immune system can help you to stay healthy and not give your immune system an opportunity to turn against you. Many antioxidants also have anti-inflammatory properties.

There are many nutrients in a healthy diet that have antioxidant properties, including several vitamins and minerals. The most well known are vitamins A, C and E. Minerals such as zinc, iron and selenium are also antioxidants.

Although vitamin A is found in dairy foods, it's better to increase your intake of beta carotene; it's a nutrient that can be converted into vitamin A if you require it, but it won't overdose the body with excess vitamin A. Beta carotene belongs to a group of plant nutrients called carotenoids. These are usually found in fruits and vegetables that are red, orange or yellow in colour, but you'll also find them in green leafy vegetables and beetroot.

Let's take a look at the foods that are rich sources of these nutrients:

| Beta carotene | Vitamin C | Vitamin E |
|---|---|---|
| Carrots | Peppers | Nuts |
| Squash | Citrus fruits | Seeds |
| Apricots | Kiwi | Avocados |
| Mango | Berries | Vegetable oils |
| Cantaloupe melon | Green leafy vegetables | Wheat germ |
| **Zinc** | **Selenium** | **Iron** |
| Wholegrains | Brazil nuts | Meat |
| Shellfish | Sunflower seeds | Beans |
| Dairy foods | Brown rice | Brown rice |
| Dark cuts of meat | Seafood | Green leafy vegetables |
| Pumpkin seeds | Eggs | Eggs |

'Although any diet benefits from a rich intake of antioxidants, for those suffering with rheumatoid arthritis an antioxidant rich diet is even more therapeutic.'

## Food which may make rheumatoid arthritis worse

Some research shows increases in rheumatoid arthritis symptoms when certain foods are eaten. Karatay *et al.* (2004) found that symptoms such as stiffness, pain and the level of inflammatory markers in the blood all increased when foods which tested positive in an allergic skin prick test were eaten. In further research they also found that symptoms were aggravated when allergenic foods were included in the diet.

'While you continue to eat foods which you are knowingly or unknowingly intolerant of, these foods stimulate your immune system to create symptoms such as inflammation, and increase your requirement for antioxidants.'

## Common food allergens

Although allergy tests may show specific foods or substances that you have an allergy to, these tests are sometimes unreliable and usually expensive. Although you may be allergic or intolerant of any food, there are some foods which cause problems much more frequently than others:

- Dairy foods, including milk, yoghurt and cheese (particularly cow's milk and cow's milk products).
- Wheat products e.g. bread and pasta.
- Gluten, a type of protein found in cereals such as wheat, oats and rye.
- Eggs.
- Citrus fruits.
- Coffee.
- Chocolate.

## Exclusion diets

If you suspect that some foods are exacerbating your arthritis, you might want to exclude them from your diet.

The first step is to remove suspect foods and/or common allergens (substances that create an allergic reaction) from your diet. Ideally, an allergen should be excluded for three weeks to allow all traces to be removed from the body, although you may notice a difference immediately or within a few days. When trying to identify a food allergen, you can exclude more than one food simultaneously by removing all suspected foods at once, but you must re-introduce each food individually otherwise it is impossible to know which food may be aggravating your symptoms.

The second stage is to re-introduce foods back into the diet and monitor your symptoms. If a food appears to cause no symptoms, you can keep it in your diet. If symptoms return or worsen, you then need to decide whether you want to continue eating that food, with the resulting symptoms, or exclude it from your diet.

During the exclusion diet, it's a good idea to keep a food diary to see how certain foods affect your arthritis. Mark each common symptom, such as stiffness or pain, from one to five so that you can measure the effects of excluding and then re-introducing foods in your diet. There is an exclusion diet in chapter 7 to help get you started.

It is best to consult a nutritionist or dietitian before excluding any major food or food group from your diet to avoid creating nutrient deficiencies and to ensure that your diet is balanced. If you are breastfeeding, pregnant or taking any medication, you should also consult with your GP before making any dietary changes. It can be difficult to remove all traces of some substances, as products from milk, eggs and wheat are added to many processed foods. A qualified practitioner will help you to plan an effective exclusion diet that is also healthy and balanced, and not lacking in any nutrients.

# The anti-inflammatory diet

Joint inflammation is a key symptom in both types of arthritis, and this is the main symptom of arthritis that may be alleviated through diet.

There are several foods that contain nutrients with anti-inflammatory properties:

- Fish.
- Nuts, seeds and their oils.
- Onions.
- Green leafy vegetables.

# Adjusting your fatty acid profile

The types of fats that we eat contribute to our natural anti-inflammatory and pro-inflammatory pathways, and in good health these are balanced. However, an imbalanced intake of fats over a period of time can cause us to be overly 'inflammatory', and so arthritis, which is an inflammatory condition, may benefit from an anti-inflammatory diet. One of the key elements of such a diet is re-balancing the types of fats that you eat.

As the only naturally rich sources of anti-inflammatory omega 3 fatty acids are fish, algae, walnuts and linseeds and their related oils, many people, especially non-fish eaters, struggle to include enough of these essential fats in their diet. Although many foods contain omega 3 and omega 6 fatty acids, very few have a healthy omega 3 to omega 6 ratio, so over time it is possible to have an unbalanced fatty acid intake as shown below:

| Diet | Ratio of omega 6 to omega 3 |
|------|------------------------------|
| Normal healthy ratio | 3:1 |
| Typical Western diet ratio | 16-20:1 |

After following such a diet for a number of years, many of us need to adjust the ratio in favour of omega 3 to correct the imbalance and reduce inflammatory conditions. As both types of fatty acids affect our inflammatory pathways, if we have too much of one type of fat and not enough of the other, we often experience symptoms such as the inflammation common to arthritis. We need lots of different nutrients to ensure that these pathways are effective, but consuming a correct ratio of essential fatty acids in your diet is a good place to start.

Check the lists below to see if you are eating enough omega 3 and omega 6.

| Foods rich in omega 3 | Foods rich in omega 6 |
|------------------------|------------------------|
| Oily fish | Margarine |
| Linseeds (flaxseeds) | Vegetable oil |
| Walnuts | Nuts and seeds |

Most seeds and nuts contain both types of fat, but usually contain more of the omega 6 fats. This table shows the omega 3 and omega 6 fatty acid contents of some nuts, seeds and oils. Remember: to reduce inflammatory symptoms, you need more omega 3 oils and fewer omega 6.

| Food | Omega 3 (g/100g) | Omega 6 (g/100g) |
|---|---|---|
| Linseed/linseed oil | 51.5 | 13 |
| Walnut | 7 | 36 |
| Brazil nut | 0 | 23.5 |
| Almonds | 0.3 | 10 |
| Sunflower seeds | 0.14 | 24.6 |
| Sunflower oil | 0.27 | 46.8 |
| Olive oil | 0.6 | 9.9 |
| Rapeseed oil | 9.3 | 18.5 |

All figures are for uncooked foods.

(Source: statistics are sourced from Food Standards Agency, 2002. © Crown Copyright and The Vegetarian Society.)

**Omega 3-rich oils**

- Olive oil is not particularly rich in omega 3 fats, but it contains considerably less omega 6 fats than other oils.

- Rapeseed oil is a rich source of omega 3 fats and also has less than half the amount of omega 6 fats found in other vegetable oils such as sunflower oil.

- Linseed oil contains an even lower proportion of omega 6 fats and has the highest amount of omega 3 oils available in a vegetable oil.

Our body fat is made up of the type of fatty acids we commonly eat, so if you have eaten very little oily fish, linseeds or walnuts over a number of years, your body fat may contain an unbalanced ratio of fatty acids. Whenever you break down your body fat for energy, the fatty acids are released into the bloodstream, so don't expect to correct a fatty acid imbalance overnight. If you think this applies to you, avoid foods such as sunflower seeds which contain more omega 6 fats than omega 3, as this will slow down your efforts to correct your fatty acid imbalance and reduce inflammation in the body.

Ways to add omega 3-rich linseeds, walnuts and oils to your diet include:

- Adding linseeds and walnuts to cereals, yoghurts, salads and stir-fries.

- Trying bars with added seeds such as the 9Bar with linseeds and chocolate.

- Just nibbling on walnuts.

- Cooking with olive oil.

- Adding rapeseed oil, walnut oil, edible linseed oil or olive oil to salads.

## Meat versus fish

Meats are rich in omega 6 fatty acids and as these acids encourage our pro-inflammatory pathways, eating too much meat may promote inflammatory responses. If you have consumed more meat than fish over a number of years, you may find it beneficial to swap your ratio around – for example, eating more fish than meat, or even omitting meat from your diet for a while. The Department of Health recommends eating two portions of oily fish per week for women and girls who may one day have a baby and four portions per week for boys and men.

Ways to swap pro-inflammatory foods for anti-inflammatory foods can include:

- Swap meat, eggs or cheese for fresh or tinned fish in sandwiches.

- Swap cheese on toast to sardines on toast.

- Swap omelette or eggs for breakfast to kedgeree or kippers.

- Swap roast meats at dinner for salmon or tuna steak.

- Use tuna or soya mince in place of mince in pasta dishes.

# Other anti-inflammatory foods and spices

## Onions

Onions (white, red, shallots, spring – any type in fact!) contain a plant nutrient called quercetin, which belongs to the flavonoid family. Flavonoids have so many health benefits they are sometimes referred to as 'Vitamin P'. As well as being anti-inflammatory, onions are also known to be:

- Anti-histamine.
- Anti-viral.
- Anti-bacterial.
- Anti-allergic.

## Green leafy vegetables

These types of vegetables contain some omega 3 fatty acids and they are also a rich source of calcium and magnesium, which can have a calmative effect within the body. Green leafy vegetables also contain antioxidant nutrients such as iron, beta carotene and vitamin C, which all support immune function.

## Spices – turmeric and ginger

Curcumin is the main active constituent in the spice turmeric. Numerous studies have illustrated its anti-inflammatory properties and it has been shown to reduce the action of collagenase, the enzyme that breaks down cartilage. In studies on joint inflammation, it appears to be most effective as a preventative measure or as an early treatment to reduce inflammation.

Include more of these anti-inflammatory foods in your diet by:

- Adding onions, rocket, watercress and spinach to sandwiches, wraps and salads.
- Adding watercress or rocket to rice and pasta dishes.
- Starting stir-fries, casseroles, stews and soups off with an onion.
- Adding onion and green leaves to omelettes.

'Shiitake mushrooms contain beta glucan which enhances immune function. Add to miso soup or sauté with onions, garlic, tofu, bean sprouts and mange tout for a healthy stir-fry.'

- Adding turmeric to stews, curries, chillies and casseroles.

- Adding ginger to desserts or soups.

- Drinking ginger tea.

There is an anti-inflammatory seven-day eating plan in chapter 7.

# Osteoarthritis

Osteoarthritis is also known as degenerative joint disease because the condition is due to the increased break down of the joints, specifically the cartilage on the ends of the bones that normally stops bones rubbing together. Although there is a gap between the bones filled with lubricating fluid, the cartilage still aids joint movement. Osteoarthritis usually affects weight-bearing joints such as the hips and knees.

Risk factors for osteoarthritis include:

- Prolonged wear and tear or overuse of joints, particularly weight-bearing joints.

- Uneven weight bearing or unbalanced joint positioning.

- There may be high levels of collagenase present (an enzyme that breaks down the collagen that forms cartilage).

- Inflammation from bony outgrowths may cause uneven loading.

## Dietary adjustments to help with osteoarthritis

Carbohydrate and protein foods largely make up our cartilage. Osteoarthritis is due to an exaggerated break down of cartilage, but simply eating more carbohydrates and protein won't have an effect – your body will just use the additional foods for other purposes, or use the excess for body fat, exacerbating the condition. It is unlikely that your diet is lacking in protein or carbohydrate, so it is likely that the break down of cartilage is due to wear and tear or enzyme-related. However, you may be able to reduce the inflammation in your joints by following the anti-inflammatory diet suggested for rheumatoid arthritis – see chapter 7.

# Supplements to help arthritis

### Glucosamine and chondroitin sulphate

Glucosamine and chondroitin sulphate are the most common types of supplement taken for osteoarthritis. These supplements contain the nutrients we use to form cartilage in the body. Glucosamine is an amino sugar that the body produces and distributes in cartilage and other connective tissue, and chondroitin sulphate is a complex carbohydrate that helps cartilage retain water.

Some arthritis sufferers report positive results after taking these supplements. However, in the large-scale glucosamine/chondroitin arthritis intervention trial (GAIT) in the US, the effects of glucosamine hydrochloride and chondroitin sulphate were tested over 24 weeks, and only those with moderate to severe pain experienced pain relief (Sawitzke AD et al., 2008). Extended research to study improvements in knee cartilage over two years with 581 participants showed no reduction in the loss of knee cartilage.

### Methyl sulphonyl methane

Methyl sulphonyl methane (MSM) is often used in conjunction with chondroitin or glucosamine. It seems to increase the effectiveness of these supplements and also helps to ease pain. In a systematic review of published research on foods and supplements affecting osteoarthritis, good evidence was found for avocado soya bean extracts and moderate evidence that MSM provides symptom relief to osteoarthritic patients (Ameye and Chee, 2008).

### Rose hip powder

Several studies indicate that rose hip powder may relieve joint pain and could offer a natural alternative to anti-inflammatory pain-killers.

### New Zealand green-lipped mussels

Although still inconclusive with mixed reports regarding the effectiveness of this supplement, some research has illustrated that green-lipped mussels may help reduce the inflammatory effects in both types of arthritis.

### Fish oils

Cod liver oil is a well-known remedy for joint problems. However, although cod liver oil is a fish oil, there are several reasons why other fish oils may be a better choice, namely eicosapentaenoic acid (EPA) and docosahexaenoic acid (DHA) fish oils.

- Fish such as cod store much of their fat along with vitamin A in the liver, and vitamin A is therefore present in most cod liver oil supplements. However, although vitamin A is essential in our diet, high intakes can be detrimental to health, and vitamin A supplementation is safer in the form of beta carotene (found in red, yellow and orange fruits and vegetables – see page 123).

- As the liver is used to detoxify the body, high levels of contaminants such as mercury or polychlorinated biphenyls (PCBs – manmade toxic chemicals) may be present in cod liver oil supplements, although these pollutants can occur in fish oil supplements even if the oils have been extracted from the flesh of the fish rather than the liver. Health risks from PCBs include cancer and damage to the immune and reproductive systems, although this is usually following long-term exposure to high levels.

- It is the anti-inflammatory properties of fish oils that may help to reduce inflammation. Cod liver oil capsules do not contain the same levels of EPA and DHA omega 3 oils, making them less effective than fish oil supplements.

If you are taking any medication, you should always check with your GP before taking any supplements. It is also recommended that you consult a qualified nutritional practitioner to help you adjust your diet and decide upon the right supplementation.

'Essential fatty acids are also thought to play a role in calcium absorption and metabolism in the body, so a fish oil supplement may also benefit osteoporosis.'

## Osteoporosis

In osteoporosis, the bones are more porous due to a lack of calcium phosphate (a compound needed to make strong bones). This makes them more liable to fracture easily, although there are often no symptoms until a fracture occurs. Up to 40% of women may suffer with osteoporosis by age 80, but the condition can be delayed or even reduced through diet and exercise.

The most effective prevention is to maximise bone mineral density while bone tissue is still forming (before age 35) with weight-bearing exercise and a balanced diet (see below).

Risk factors for osteoporosis can include:

- Lack of regular weight-bearing exercise or long periods of immobility.

- Very low body weight.

- Age, race and gender (osteoporosis becomes more common as we age, in those of black African Caribbean origin and in post-menopausal women).

- Reduced levels of hormones such as oestrogen or testosterone which promote bone building.

- Other medical conditions such as rheumatoid arthritis, hyperthyroidism (overactive thyroid), parathyroid disease (disorder of the parathyroid gland), or malabsorption conditions such as Crohn's disease.

- Smoking.

- Long-term use of corticosteroids and some medications used for breast or prostate cancer.

- Drinking coffee.

- Drinking more than three units of alcohol a day.

- Drinking fizzy drinks.

- Excessive salt intake.

- Excessive protein intake.

- Lack of essential nutrients such as calcium and vitamin D in the diet, or malabsorption of nutrients (which means you are eating enough, but just not absorbing enough into your body).

## Exercise and osteoporosis

We build bone tissue as required, so the more regularly we place a certain amount of strain on the bones, the more that bone tissue is laid down to make the skeletal structure stronger. With a sedentary lifestyle not even involving much walking around, bone tissue will reduce and weaken, sometimes leading to osteoporosis. Although it is advisable to strengthen the bones before the age of 35, it's never too late to start a weight-bearing exercise regime. Weight-bearing exercise is activity that requires the body, or parts of the body, to take the strain of your body weight, or work against the resistance of weights or resistance bands. Here are some examples of weight-bearing exercise – ideally you need to do one of these at least four to five times weekly.

- Walking and hiking.

- Jogging or running.

- Stair climbing.

- Gym machines such as the cross trainer or stepper.

- Yoga or Tai chi.

- Weight training.

- Fitness or dance classes.

However, too much exercise or insufficient food intake leading to a low, unhealthy body weight will contribute to osteoporosis. This is because the body begins to take essential nutrients from the bones, which weakens them.

## How age and gender affects our bones

Although we can affect how much bone tissue is laid down with regular exercise, our hormone levels alter as we age, and this also affects our bones. Some hormones promote the lay down of tissues such as bone, so when levels of these hormones reduce, less bone tissue is formed. Hormones such as oestrogen affect our bones in this way, which is why reducing amounts of oestrogen during and after the menopause increases the risk of osteoporosis.

This can be partially offset by replacing the natural oestrogens with plant oestrogens called phytoestrogens. These nutrients affect our cells in a more subtle but similar way to natural oestrogen. Studies have looked at the low rates of osteoporosis (and breast cancer) in Japanese women who traditionally consume high levels of phytoestrogens in their diet. Compare this to the higher rates of these diseases in the UK, where we eat fewer phytoestrogen-rich foods, and the research suggests that we may benefit from eating more phytoestrogen-rich foods.

Foods rich in phytoestrogens include:

- Soya products such as soya beans, soya milk, soya yoghurt and tofu.
- Chickpeas, lentils and mung beans.
- Fruits such as apples, plums and cherries.
- Peppers, yams, tomatoes, olives, carrots, fennel, potatoes and aubergine.

Some ideas to add phytoestrogen-rich food to your diet could be:

- Adding soya yoghurt, plums, cherries and apples to breakfast.
- Replacing dairy milk with soya milk.
- Snacking on plums, cherries, apples, olives, peppers and carrots.
- Adding tofu to stir-fries.
- Filling up on lentil soup.
- Adding chickpeas to salads, curries and stir-fries.
- Snacking on hummus (made with chickpeas).
- Using frozen soya beans as a vegetable staple.

## How your diet affects your bones

As osteoporosis is a condition identified by porous bones, any foods or drinks that may increase mineral loss from the bones will contribute to the condition. There are several dietary habits that can contribute to bone loss:

- Coffee consumption.
- Alcohol consumption.
- Consuming fizzy drinks.
- Too much salt.
- Too much protein.

▪ Not enough bone-building nutrients.

### Coffee

Coffee has a diuretic effect upon the body – it makes us produce more urine. While this is a natural mechanism, whenever we form urine essential minerals such as calcium and magnesium may be lost. If these minerals remain in the bloodstream, they are available to be laid down as bone tissue. However, if lost in urine production, calcium in particular is then drawn out of the bones to replenish the calcium lost from the bloodstream. Tea does not appear to have the same effect.

Calcium loss is likely to increase in line with coffee consumption, so try to limit your cups of coffee to no more than three cups daily, or maybe swap to tea.

### Alcohol

Alcohol intake has been linked with decreased bone density, and therefore higher risk of osteoporosis. There appears to be no detrimental effect when alcohol intake is low; in fact, some studies have shown better bone density in those that drink sparingly than those that drink nothing at all. However, drinking more than one drink daily affects the intake, absorption and metabolism of nutrients such as zinc and leads to poor bone structure.

### Fizzy drinks

Calcium phosphate is the main component of bone tissue, but as with all things in life, too much of a good thing isn't always good for us! Phosphate is present in many foods, and added to fizzy drinks (as phosphoric acid) and processed foods. Your body monitors calcium and phosphate levels closely and any excess are excreted in urine. Drinking fizzy drinks may result in too much phosphorus in the blood, and as a result calcium will be excreted with the phosphorus through urine – potentially leading to a calcium deficiency. The best way to reduce your phosphorus intake is to replace fizzy drinks with milk, juice or water, which all offer multiple nutritional benefits.

'Although mechanisms are in place to reabsorb calcium and magnesium if they are needed, drinking approximately eight cups of coffee daily can increase mineral loss in the urine.'

## Salt

The amount of salt in our diet affects the amount of water we retain in our bloodstream – high salt levels lead to elevated blood pressure. Fluid and salt levels are closely controlled by the kidneys. If there is too much salt in the bloodstream, this can lead to higher calcium and magnesium losses in the urine, which reduces availability of these minerals for bone formation.

Current recommendations from the Food Standards Agency are to not exceed 6g of salt a day, but you should preferably aim for less. At present, the average intake in the UK is approximately 9g per day. One way to offset the effects of excess salt and reduce calcium loss in urine is to consume plenty of potassium, found in fruits, vegetables and juices. For more tips on how to reduce your salt intake, refer back to chapter 1.

## Protein

Although we require protein to make strong bones, too much protein in the diet can result in loss of calcium and magnesium salts being taken out of the bone as these minerals are used to buffer the acidity in the blood created by the protein. A healthy diet should provide approximately 60% of our food energy from carbohydrate foods, 20-25% from fats and 15-20% from protein-rich foods such as meat, fish, eggs, dairy foods (milk, cheese and yoghurt) and soya.

## Nutrients

In addition to protein, bone tissue is mostly made up of calcium, phosphorus and magnesium, but several vitamins and minerals are required for the healthy manufacture and sustenance of bone. These nutrients and the foods they are found in are listed below.

- Calcium – essential for bone formation and can be found in dairy products, dark green leafy vegetables, seeds, beans and tinned sardines.

- Phosphorus – needed for the formation of calcium phosphate, the main constituent of bone. Phosphorus is present in most processed foods and fizzy drinks.

'Our blood needs to remain close to neutral (a pH value of 7.4, where 1 is a strong acid and 14 is a strong alkali), so any drop in pH needs correcting by "buffers" such as calcium.'

- Magnesium – deficiency of this mineral increases your risk of osteoporosis as it works in conjunction with calcium and helps vitamin D production. It is found in leafy vegetables, cauliflower, seeds, nuts, pulses and dairy produce.

- Vitamin D – needed for calcium and phosphorus absorption and metabolism; we make approximately 90% of our vitamin D requirements in response to sun exposure. As we make most of our vitamin D in the summer, it's essential that we store enough to get us through winter, although we can still make some vitamin D on cloudy days. Sun block will prevent vitamin D production, but only 15 to 20 minutes of sun exposure to the arms and face three to four times weekly is required to make enough vitamin D for the year. Vitamin D is also found in oily fish, fortified margarines and cereals.

'If you are housebound or cover your skin for cultural or religious reasons, you may benefit from a vitamin D supplement.'

- Zinc – helps to regulate bone tissue growth. It can be found in wholegrains, meat, pumpkin seeds, liver, wheat germ, Brazil and pecan nuts, shellfish and oysters.

- Vitamin C – helps in collagen formation to maintain bone strength, and also enhances iron absorption. Vitamin C can be found in berries, peppers, tomatoes, potatoes, dark green leafy vegetables and citrus fruit.

- Vitamin K – helps to form proteins used in building bone and aids in bone healing. People with osteoporosis often have low levels of vitamin K, suggesting it may have preventative qualities. Vitamin K is found in green leafy vegetables, broccoli, cauliflower and soya beans.

- Copper – nearly 20% of the body's copper is in the bones where it helps to build bone tissue. It can be found in nuts and seeds, mushrooms, crab and fruit.

- Manganese – lack of manganese can cause osteoporosis. It is present in leafy vegetables, nuts, seeds, meat, pulses and wholegrains.

- Silicon – keeps bones and connective tissues healthy, and may increase bone density. Found in oats, barley and rice.

- Boron – has been shown to reduce the levels of calcium excreted via urine and increase oestrogen levels. Found in nuts, dairy products, apples, pears, grapes and green leafy vegetables.

With a long list like this, it's clear you need to eat a healthy, balanced diet for good bone health, as shown in the eatwell plate overleaf.

The eatwell plate shows how much of what you eat should come from each food group. For good bone health, it's essential to eat:

- Plenty of fruit and vegetables.
- Adequate amounts of wholegrain bread, rice, pasta and potatoes.
- Some milk and dairy foods.
- Some meat, fish, eggs, beans and other non-dairy sources of protein.
- Only a small amount of high fat/sugary foods and fizzy drinks.

## Poor nutrient absorption

Although some foods are rich in calcium, they also contain substances such as phytates or oxalates, which bind to calcium and hinder its absorption into the body. This shouldn't be a problem as long as all of your calcium isn't coming from foods that contain lots of phytates or oxalates – underlining the importance of a varied diet. Oxalates are high in spinach and rhubarb, so although these foods contain lots of calcium, most of it is unavailable as the oxalic acid connects to it and stops it being absorbed into the body. Phytates are found in bran and the outside of wholegrains, so eating these foods at the same time as calcium-rich foods might reduce the amount of calcium you absorb. These foods are still a healthy addition to your diet, but just make sure that you also eat foods such as tinned fish with bones, enriched soya products, other green leafy vegetables and dairy products to ensure adequate calcium intake.

# The eatwell plate

Use the eatwell plate to help you get the balance right. It shows how much of what you eat should come from each food group.

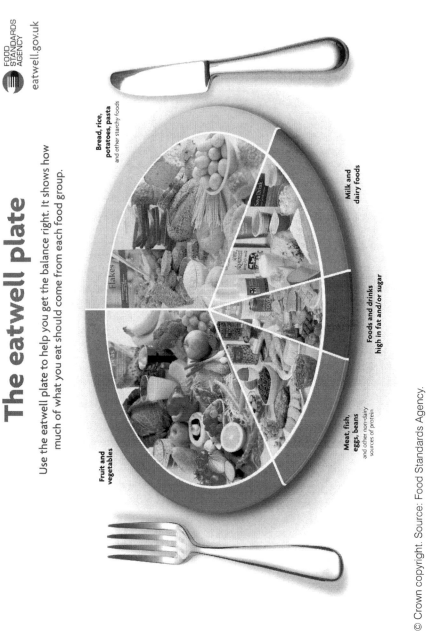

FOOD STANDARDS AGENCY

eatwell.gov.uk

Bread, rice, potatoes, pasta and other starchy foods

Milk and dairy foods

Foods and drinks high in fat and/or sugar

Meat, fish, eggs, beans and other non-dairy sources of protein

Fruit and vegetables

© Crown copyright. Source: Food Standards Agency.

© Crown copyright material is reproduced with the permission of the Controller of HMSO and Queen's Printer of Scotland.

# Summing Up

To help avoid or combat arthritis:

- Include anti-inflammatory foods such as fish, linseeds, onions and green leafy vegetables in your diet.

- Consider an exclusion diet to avoid foods you may be intolerant of.

- Eat a diet rich in antioxidants to combat inflammation and support immune function.

- Include anti-inflammatory spices such as turmeric and ginger.

To help avoid or combat osteoporosis:

- Base meals on bone building nutrients from nuts, seeds, beans and pulses, fruit and vegetables, fish and soya or dairy produce.

- Limit coffee, fizzy drinks and alcohol.

- Cut down on salt.

- Give up smoking.

- Avoid high protein diets.

- Try to stay active and maintain a healthy body weight.

- Get some sunshine!

## Help avoid or combat arthritis

| Stick to... | Stay away from... |
| --- | --- |
| Fish. | Meat. |
| Nuts and seeds, especially walnuts/ linseeds. | Omega 6-rich sunflower oils. |
| Green leafy vegetables. | Suspect foods or common allergens. |
| Shiitake mushrooms. | |
| Antioxidant-rich foods. | |
| Turmeric and ginger. | |
| Onions. | |

## Help avoid or combat osteoporosis

| Stick to... | Stay away from... |
| --- | --- |
| Soya foods. | High-protein diets. |
| Protein-rich meat, fish, dairy produce and eggs. | Fizzy drinks. |
| Fruit and vegetables. | Alcohol. |
| Nuts and seeds. | Salt. |
| Wholegrains and beans. | Caffeine. |

# Chapter Three

## Sweet But Deadly

Many of us live on a blood sugar roller coaster, going from one quick fix to the next, with blood sugar highs created by cups of coffee and sugary, refined-carbohydrate snacks (like chocolate, cakes and pastries), alternating with slumps in energy. Sound familiar?

However, although we have natural mechanisms to help control our blood sugar levels, a poor diet which consistently takes our body to blood sugar extremes is detrimental to continued good health.

## Blood sugar and insulin

Whenever we consume quick-release carbohydrates that raise our blood sugar levels, we produce a hormone called insulin which reduces the level of sugar (glucose) in our bloodstream. It does this in a number of ways:

- Insulin increases the amount of glucose that goes into the cells.
- Insulin increases the conversion of glucose into glycogen (its storage form in the liver and muscles).
- Insulin decreases fat break down for energy so that we can utilise excess glucose instead.
- Insulin stimulates the conversion of excess glucose into fat.

Insulin is required to move the glucose into our cells so that we can use it for energy. If high levels of glucose remain in the bloodstream, not only is it useless as an energy supply, but it also damages important proteins that are travelling in the bloodstream, affecting our health in a number of ways as these proteins become denatured (destroyed) and ineffective.

High sugar levels result in your body releasing more insulin to reduce the blood sugar, but sometimes this means sugar levels fall again and you crave more caffeine, sugar or quick-release carbohydrates. This can create blood sugar highs and lows throughout the day, increasing your need for sugar and stimulants, which in turn tends to lower your intake of wholesome, nutritious foods.

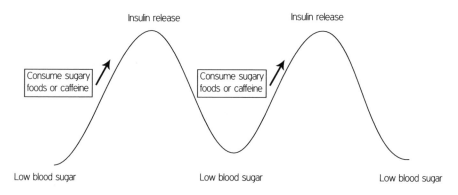

Often, when we have the urge to consume something sweet, these foods also contain high levels of fat or calories. Foods such as sweets, biscuits, doughnuts, chocolate and pastries are commonly used to elevate blood sugar level, so when considering food intake for the day, you are likely to think you have eaten very little as these snacks are not considered as meals. The danger of snacking on these types of foods is that you often underestimate your calorie intake, which can lead to weight gain and increase the risk of diabetes and heart disease.

A further problem associated with sugary snacks is that they are unlikely to be rich sources of vitamins and minerals, so your diet may be lacking in vital nutrients needed for health and energy.

## What are carbohydrates?

Although foods are classed as carbohydrates, proteins and fats, most foods are a combination of more than one of these. However, it's the carbohydrate-rich foods that affect our blood sugar levels the most. The term carbohydrate encompasses starchy carbohydrates like rice, pasta and potatoes (what we typically think of as carbohydrates), but also non-starchy carbohydrates like fruits and vegetables.

# Sugars, starches and non-starch polysaccharides

All carbohydrate foods contain varying amounts of sugars and/or starches. A sugar is a simple molecule that is absorbed quickly into the bloodstream; glucose is one of these sugars, and it is glucose that we use for energy.

The starches are made up of sugar molecules all joined together to make larger molecules called polysaccharides. Some polysaccharides form fibre which we don't digest, found in higher amounts in the non-starch polysaccharides (fruits and vegetables). Other polysaccharide chains form starches (found in the starchy carbohydrate foods such as rice and potatoes) which take longer to be broken down, digested and absorbed into the bloodstream. This means that polysaccharides tend to give us a more sustained release of energy, rather than creating the quick surge of energy that foods high in sugars provide.

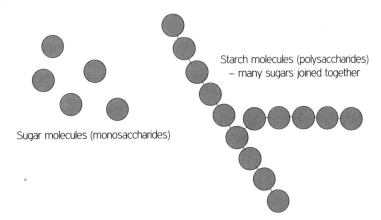

Starch molecules (polysaccharides) – many sugars joined together

Sugar molecules (monosaccharides)

Glucose itself requires no digestion and is absorbed quickly, raising blood sugar levels. Although other sugars (also known as monosaccharides) such as fructose (found in fruits) or galactose (found in milk products) are also absorbed quickly, they do not have the same immediate effect upon our blood sugar levels.

Foods rich in sugars (monosaccharides):

- Jams and marmalade.
- Sugar and syrups.

Foods rich in fibre (non-starch polysaccharides):

- Fruits (which also contain natural sugars).
- Vegetables (which also contain some starch polysaccharides which we can digest for energy).

Carbohydrate-rich foods containing more starchy polysaccharides:

- Potatoes.
- Rice.
- Beans and pulses.
- Breakfast cereals.
- Bread.
- Pasta.

## Glycaemic index

The glycaemic index (GI) is a scale of 1-100 indicating how quickly the glucose (sugar) in carbohydrate-rich foods is absorbed into the bloodstream – a low GI will mean the food has low glucose content or contains mostly slow-release starches. A high-GI score indicates a food that will give you energy more quickly. You can choose to eat certain foods based upon their GI to provide you with a more sustained energy release or a quick burst of energy.

Different food brands, cooking methods and even the stage of ripeness alter the GI of foods, but the table below illustrates the average GI of many common foods.

| Food | GI | Food | GI |
|------|-----|------|-----|
| Rice cakes | 77 | Rye crispbread | 63 |
| Easy cook white rice | 87 | Brown rice | 55 |

| White baguette | 95 | Pumpernickel bread | 50 |
|---|---|---|---|
| Gluten-free bread | 90 | Oatcakes | 54 |
| White bread | 70 | Rye bread | 51 |
| Couscous | 65 | Chickpeas | 28 |
| Puffed wheat | 80 | Porridge | 49 |
| Parsnips | 97 | Cauliflower | 0 |
| Rice pudding | 81 | Fruit yoghurt | 33 |
| Watermelon | 72 | Grapefruit | 25 |
| Pineapple | 59 | Cherries | 22 |
| Chocolate ice cream | 68 | Strawberry mousse | 32 |
| Fizzy orange drink | 68 | Apple juice | 40 |

## Glycaemic load

The glycaemic load (GL) of a food gives a value according to the effect that a normal portion will have on your blood sugar levels. It relates to the type of carbohydrate in a food (the GI) and how much carbohydrate a typical portion contains. It can be calculated as follows:

$$\frac{\text{Glycaemic index (GI) x the weight (g) of carbohydrate to be eaten}}{100}$$

If you check a food label for carbohydrate grams, the higher the grams per portion, the higher the GL. If a food has a high GI as well, it will give you a quicker release of energy because the carbohydrates are sugars and readily absorbed.

Although the GI indicates whether a food or drink contains a high proportion of glucose, not all high-GI foods contain large amounts of glucose. For example, water melon has a reasonably high GI as most of the sugars are glucose. However, it doesn't have a high GL as so much of it is water; a typical portion contains only 14g of carbohydrate, in comparison to 40g in a 250ml bottle of Lucozade.

'Riper fruits and vegetables will have a higher GI – a ripe banana contains more sugars than a starchy green banana.'

Large and frequent highs and lows in blood sugar levels caused by high-GI foods can affect your body's ability to manage blood sugar levels properly, potentially leading to hypoglycaemic (low blood sugar) conditions or even diabetes.

# Diabetes and pre-diabetic conditions

Diabetes is an increasing global health problem. According to Diabetes UK, there are currently over 2.5 million people with diabetes in the UK, and up to half a million people with undiagnosed diabetes, with pre-diabetic conditions such as insulin resistance, metabolic syndrome and low blood sugar commonplace. Diabetes is diagnosed if you have an average fasting blood glucose (sugar) level of 7mmol/L (millimoles per litre of blood). Fasting (no food or drink for eight hours) blood glucose levels of more than 6.1mmol/L are an indication of impaired blood sugar regulation and defects in insulin metabolism.

Diabetes mellitus is a group of metabolic diseases characterised by high blood sugar levels due to defects in the body's insulin production. Diabetes mellitus means 'sweet urine', named as such because high blood sugar levels result in excess sugar being excreted in the urine. Although the term 'diabetes' is commonly used as an umbrella term, there are several different types of diabetes, although Type 1 and Type 2 are the most common. Additional information on other types of diabetes can be found at www.diabetes.co.uk.

## Risk factors

Your risk of diabetes is greater if there is already diabetes in the family. It also depends on race (African-Caribbean or South Asian people are at least five times more likely to have diabetes), and occurrence increases with age. Diagnosed conditions such as coronary heart disease and polycystic ovarian syndrome also increase the risk of diabetes, as does poor blood sugar regulation (diagnosed as impaired fasting glycaemia or impaired glucose tolerance, which both indicate high blood sugar levels). Other conditions such as raised levels of fats in the blood and severe mental health problems can also increase your risk.

There are several lifestyle elements under your control that can increase your risk of diabetes:

- Excess body weight, particularly around the middle (central obesity).
- Eating too many sugary foods and refined carbohydrate foods.
- Drinking too much alcohol.
- Smoking.

The more risk factors that apply to you, the greater your risk of developing diabetes and other conditions with impaired blood sugar control.

## Type 1 diabetes

Type 1 diabetes (also known as insulin-dependent or juvenile diabetes) is less common than Type 2 diabetes. It is an autoimmune condition, where the body's immune system destroys the beta cells (which produce insulin) in the pancreas, meaning that the body can no longer produce insulin to regulate blood sugar levels. Type 1 diabetes is usually diagnosed in childhood. Although the symptoms of Type 1 diabetes can be affected by diet and exercise, it cannot be reversed or cured, and blood sugar regulation relies upon regular insulin injections.

## Type 2 diabetes

Type 2 diabetes is also called non-insulin-dependent diabetes, adult-onset or late-onset diabetes. However, with increasing levels of obesity and bad eating habits, it is now also found in young adults and children.

In Type 2 diabetes, either the pancreas does not produce enough insulin to reduce blood sugar levels or the insulin fails to have the required effect upon the cells, so blood sugar is not reduced. Therefore, characteristics of this disease include insulin deficiency and/or insulin resistance, with the result of too much insulin in the bloodstream (hyperinsulinaemia) and high blood sugar levels (hyperglycaemia). Type 2 diabetes can sometimes be controlled with diet and exercise, but if blood sugar levels fail to be stabilised, various medications and eventually insulin therapy are used.

## Reactive and fasting hypoglycaemia

Hypoglycaemia is low blood sugar. Although high blood sugar is the main problem in most pre-diabetic and diabetic conditions, regular low blood sugar may be a contributory cause of these conditions, as it is caused by common practices such as:

- Missing meals.

- Following low-calorie diets.

- Eating sugary foods, resulting in high insulin release and subsequent low blood sugar levels (which usually leads to eating more sugary foods).

None of these practices contribute to healthy blood sugar regulation, and repeated low blood sugar can create conditions known as fasting and reactive hypoglycaemia.

Fasting hypoglycaemia is a condition where blood sugar levels tend to remain low, creating symptoms of hypoglycaemia such as tiredness, inability to concentrate, sugar cravings and feeling faint. A sugary or high carbohydrate diet results in greater insulin production, which initially causes low blood sugar levels. However, it can develop into a condition known as reactive hypoglycaemia, where too much insulin is released, and over time may cause the cells to become resistant to insulin.

## Insulin resistance

Too many sugary or quick-release (high GI) carbohydrates can over-stimulate insulin release, and over time cells can become 'resistant' to insulin. Many Type 2 diabetics and those with polycystic ovarian syndrome, pre-diabetes and metabolic syndrome suffer from a condition known as insulin resistance. This is where insulin is still released from the pancreas, but the cells do not respond to it. If insulin cannot 'open the gates' to enable sugar to enter body cells, the sugar remains in the bloodstream and creates high blood sugar (hyperglycaemia). Because the blood sugar levels remain high, the pancreas may continue to produce insulin, leading to high blood insulin levels as well (hyperinsulinaemia).

54

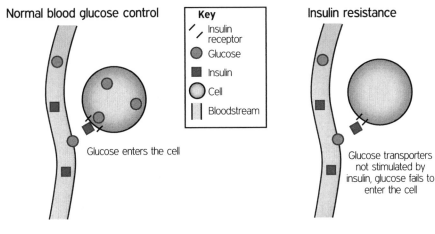

Normal blood glucose control

**Key**
- ⁄ ⁄ Insulin receptor
- ⬤ Glucose
- ■ Insulin
- ◯ Cell
- ‖ Bloodstream

Glucose enters the cell

Insulin resistance

Glucose transporters not stimulated by insulin, glucose fails to enter the cell

Insulin resistance causes several health risks:

- It causes high blood sugar.

- Proteins and fats are also taken in by cells in response to insulin release. If the cells fail to respond to insulin, fat levels in the blood increase, increasing the risk of coronary heart disease.

- The increase in substances in the bloodstream (insulin, sugar, proteins and fats) results in elevated blood pressure.

- High levels of glucose in the blood 'attach' to blood proteins and damage them, rendering them useless.

- If cells cannot use the glucose for energy, it is more likely to be converted into fat in the liver, contributing to weight gain and central obesity.

So although sugary, refined carbohydrate foods may seem relatively low in calories in comparison to fats, regularly eating these foods is not a good idea for your waistline or your health.

## Metabolic syndrome

Metabolic syndrome is the combination of diabetes, high blood pressure and obesity. It's also called insulin resistance syndrome because one of the features is high insulin levels and insulin resistance. Metabolic syndrome is very common and becoming more so. You are at risk if you're overweight, inactive and have a genetic predisposition to developing metabolic syndrome (i.e. it runs in your family).

Complications from metabolic syndrome include:

- Central obesity.
- An increased tendency towards inflammatory conditions throughout the body due to the 'hormone-like' inflammatory substances secreted by abdominal fat tissue.
- High levels of fats and low levels of 'good' cholesterol in the bloodstream.
- An increased tendency to form blood clots, contributing to coronary heart disease.
- High blood pressure.
- Insulin resistance or sugar intolerance – an inability to use insulin properly or control blood sugar levels.

## Pre-diabetes

Pre-diabetes is a term used to describe consistently elevated blood glucose levels and/or impaired glucose regulation. It may also be called impaired glucose tolerance, impaired fasting glucose or non-diabetic hyperglycaemia, and increases the risk of developing Type 2 diabetes by up to 15 times.

Symptoms of pre-diabetes are high blood glucose levels and being overweight. The changes in body chemistry that lead to diabetes, such as decreased sensitivity to insulin (which means that blood glucose levels remain high), begin several years before symptoms become apparent. With such a high prevalence of blood sugar dysfunction, it seems that even if you haven't got diabetes, it's worth making lifestyle changes to ensure that blood sugar regulation stays healthy.

# Regulate your blood sugar through your diet

The food and drink that we consume every day affects our blood sugar levels and can be either helpful or detrimental to blood sugar control. There are a number of ways you can help regulate your blood sugar levels.

- Exercise for better weight control.
- Moderate carbohydrate intake.
- Use the GI or GL of foods to stabilise blood sugar levels.
- Manipulate the GI of your meals.
- Reduce the overall GL of your meals.
- Use protein and high-fibre foods to your advantage.
- Moderate alcohol consumption.
- Limit caffeinated drinks.
- Eat spices and herbs with anti-hyperglycaemic properties.

## Weight control

Over 80% of people diagnosed with Type 2 diabetes are overweight. The more overweight and the more inactive you are, the greater your risk – particularly if the excess body fat is around the middle. Central obesity decreases the liver's sensitivity to insulin, and if the liver fails to take in glucose and store it, blood sugar levels remain elevated and contribute to the development of Type 2 diabetes. You can find out if you are at increased risk by checking your waist circumference or waist-hip ratio as outlined in chapter 1.

## Moderate carbohydrate intake

As carbohydrates are formed from sugars such as glucose, it makes sense that the less carbohydrate you eat, the less glucose you will absorb. This in itself will help to reduce blood sugar levels and the amount of insulin required to control them. However, carbohydrates are an important part of the diet

'The "apple" shape is less desirable than the "pear" shape as far as health goes: body fat tissue around the abdomen is linked with increased risk of Type 2 diabetes, coronary heart disease and inflammatory endocrine disorders.'

providing energy and essential nutrients, so you should not reduce your carbohydrate levels lower than between 50-60% of your calorie intake unless advised to do so by a healthcare professional.

Remember, there is more glucose in a starchy carbohydrate (e.g. rice, pasta, cereals, potatoes, etc) than in a non-starchy carbohydrate (e.g. fruits and vegetables), so reduce your intake of starchy carbohydrates but fill up on low-GI fruits and vegetables containing less starch (and therefore less glucose) and more antioxidants.

Follow these guidelines to get your carbohydrate intake right:

- Include starchy carbohydrates in most meals, but go for a wholegrain version if you can and limit the portion size.

- Eat a wide range of different types of carbohydrate foods, and don't forget to include low-GI beans, pulses and lentils for slow-release, starchy-carbohydrate energy.

- Fill up on non-starchy carbohydrates such as fruits and vegetables.

- Choose lower GI fruits and vegetables to reduce glucose intake.

- Avoid or limit foods with a high GI, particularly sugary foods and refined carbohydrates such as biscuits, cakes, muffins and pastries.

## Using the GI or GL of foods to stabilise blood sugar levels

There are a number of ways that you can use the GI of foods to help stabilise blood sugar levels.

### Avoiding and reducing the effect of high-GI foods

You can avoid or limit foods with a high GI, eat smaller portions of high-GI foods, and/or combine these foods with low-GI foods, proteins or fatty foods to slow down the absorption of glucose into your bloodstream. Check out *Collins Gem 'GI',* a GI dictionary arranged in food groups and listing foods in a traffic light style: red for high GI, amber for medium GI and green for low GI.

## Swapping high-GI for low-GI foods

Simply swapping your higher GI foods for higher-fibre, lower GI options can make a difference to blood sugar regulation. See how many of these you can do:

- Swap white bread for wholemeal or GI bread.
- Swap white rice for brown rice.
- Swap white pasta for durum wheat pasta.
- Replace some of your starchy carbohydrates with non-starchy carbohydrates, i.e. fruit and vegetables.
- Make cakes, muffins and biscuits with less white flour and sugar – use more fruit, fructose sugar, ground almonds or wholemeal flour instead.

Swapping starchy carbohydrates for non-starchy carbohydrates will also decrease your calorie intake and help you to control your weight. It will have the added benefit of increasing the amount of antioxidants such as vitamin C and beta carotene, which help to counteract the damage done by the inflammation encountered in diabetes and heart disease.

## Manipulating the GI of your foods

Carbohydrate absorption and digestion is affected by lots of different factors:

- Eating fatty or protein foods at the same time as a carbohydrate will slow down the absorption of glucose.
- Eating high-fibre foods also slows down the absorption of glucose.
- Combining lower GI foods with high-GI foods will reduce the overall GI of your meal.
- Even if a food has a high GI, if you reduce the portion size you reduce the GL, so the amount of glucose you are consuming is lower.
- Cooking foods for longer breaks down the walls of the starch molecules – this makes the glucose more readily available and increases the GI, so al dente vegetables will be absorbed slower than vegetables cooked for a longer time.

## Reduce the overall GL of your meal

Take a look at these suggestions. If you can put any into practice, you will increase nutrients at the same time as decreasing calories and carbohydrate intake.

| What to reduce | What to add in |
|---|---|
| Reduce your portion size of cereal | Add any low-GI fruit – cherries, citrus fruits, apples, pears, cherries, prunes or strawberries. |
| Reduce your portion of rice | Add vegetables to the rice while it cooks, risotto-style. Pack it out with onions, garlic, frozen peas, peppers and sweetcorn. Alternatively, cook the rice separately but add extra vegetables to the other part of your meal, packing out chilli, curry or stroganoff with vegetables containing less starch and fewer calories. |
| Reduce your portion of pasta | Replace starchy pasta with water-rich aubergines, courgettes, tomatoes, red onions and garlic for a lower calorie and tastier Mediterranean style meal with added health benefits. |
| Have fewer potatoes | Swap potatoes for other vegetables. The bright colours of vegetables such as pumpkin, carrot, beetroot or broccoli show the high levels of nutrients in these foods, which all contain less starch and fewer calories than potatoes. |

'Grab a handful of protein-rich, low-GI nuts as a snack between meals to boost energy levels. Be careful if you're watching your calorie intake though, as nuts are a concentrated source of energy.'

We are more likely to eat a large portion of carbohydrate-rich foods than protein or fatty foods, as carbohydrates are usually very palatable and quicker to digest, particularly low-fibre, refined carbohydrates such as white bread. Simply weighing the portion size of cereal, rice or pasta can help you to reduce your carbohydrate intake and produce less insulin.

## Using protein and high-fibre foods to your advantage

Eating protein foods with carbohydrates slows down the release of glucose into the bloodstream, reducing the GI of a meal – this can help you to control blood sugar highs and lows. Foods naturally high in fibre have the same effect. Protein foods also make us feel full, reducing the likelihood of eating sugary snacks between meals. Here are some examples of combining protein foods with low-GI carbohydrates: porridge oats with added yoghurt; peppered mackerel with chickpea and mixed bean salad; brown rice with chicken, turkey, fish or tofu.

## Moderate alcohol consumption

Alcohol is made from carbohydrate food sources; wine from grapes, cider from apples, whisky from rye and beer from grains. As such, it can have similar effects to sugar intake, causing low blood sugar levels. A moderate amount of alcohol can be tolerated without causing blood sugar irregularities or ill health, if you follow these guidelines:

▪ If you are going to drink alcohol, don't drink it on its own as it will affect blood sugar levels more severely. Drink it shortly before, during or soon after a meal.

▪ Do not substitute alcoholic drinks for your usual meal or snacks as this may lead to low blood sugar, particularly if you already have difficulties controlling blood sugar levels.

▪ Serious hypoglycaemia can occur with larger quantities of alcohol, particularly if you are treated with insulin and if too little carbohydrate is eaten, so always eat some starchy carbohydrates with alcohol.

▪ Alcohol contains seven calories per gram and will contribute to weight gain, a risk factor for Type 2 diabetes.

▪ A regular high alcohol intake can elevate blood pressure and contribute to heart disease.

▪ If you have neuropathy (nerve damage), drinking alcohol can make it worse and increase the pain, tingling, numbness and other symptoms associated with nerve damage.

- Low carbohydrate beers and cider offer no benefit because of their higher alcohol content which contains more calories and is more likely to cause low blood sugar, and low alcohol wines are often higher in sugar than ordinary wine, so always moderate alcohol consumption – whatever you drink.

- Drinks with a high sugar content such as sweet wines, 'alcopops' and liqueurs should be limited due to the high sugar and calorie count.

- You could opt for 'diet' or 'sugar-free' mixers such as diet tonic water and diet cola to reduce sugar intake, although artificial sweeteners are not recommended either!

- If you do drink alcohol, then wine, especially red wine, may offer some heart-health benefits – see chapter 1 for more information.

## Don't rely on caffeinated drinks

When we consume caffeinated products, we produce adrenaline. Adrenaline is our 'fight or flight' hormone, and stimulates the conversion of stored carbohydrate into glucose, elevating blood sugar levels. This is what creates the energy surge that you experience when you have a cup of tea or coffee, or a glass of caffeinated cola.

We often use caffeine to improve our energy levels, but it can, if used too frequently, also result in energy slumps in between 'fixes'. Regular consumption of coffee (more than two or three cups daily) can result in the same blood sugar highs and lows you would experience with a regular intake of high-GI or sugary foods. Once blood sugar levels are elevated after coffee consumption, insulin is released to reduce the high level of glucose; high levels of sugar in the bloodstream can lead to difficulties in blood sugar regulation, leading to insulin resistance and diabetes.

### Healthier alternatives to tea and coffee

Various herbs and spices can help you control blood sugar levels. By replacing your usual brew with one of these, you are not only reducing the blood sugar highs from caffeine stimulation, but actually helping to improve your blood sugar control. Try some of these alternatives:

'Although a moderate amount of caffeine can provide instant energy and improve concentration, if we use caffeine as a constant pick-me-up, we risk becoming tolerant of it and needing larger amounts.'

- Green tea contains catechins which have strong antioxidant properties and have been shown to improve pancreatic function.

- Place a cinnamon stick into some hot water or skimmed milk to enjoy its anti-hyperglycaemic properties.

- Sage tea has been shown to reduce blood sugar by reducing your cells' resistance to glucose, meaning more glucose is taken into the cells.

## Spices and herbs with anti-hyperglycaemic properties

There are a number of spices and herbs that are believed to help control blood sugar levels, such as cinnamon, fenugreek and turmeric. Each spice or herb works in different ways; the important thing is that they have the potential to help you control your blood sugar levels and are tasty, nutritious and easy to add to your diet.

Try adding cinnamon to:

- Porridge and other cereals.

- Puddings such as rice pudding or bread and butter pudding.

- Baked or stewed fruit.

- Hot drinks such as herbal teas or hot chocolate – add a cinnamon stick or sprinkle in some of the spice.

Try adding turmeric to:

- Curries, chilies, stews and casseroles.

- Stir-fries, baked or roasted meats, fish or vegetables.

- Sauces or salad dressings.

- Yoghurt to make your own dip.

Add fenugreek seeds to:

- Curries or chillies.

- Stir-fries.

- Roasted or baked vegetables, meats or fish, salad (sprinkling them on top).

'While definitive conclusions cannot be drawn regarding the therapeutic use of cinnamon as an anti-diabetic therapy, there is little doubt regarding its anti-hyperglycaemic effects.'

# Summing Up

To rebalance blood sugar levels and reduce the risk of diabetes, you should try to:

- Eat high-fibre, wholegrain carbohydrates like brown rice and pulses.
- Choose low-GI foods such as oats and beans.
- Include a little protein in small, regular meals throughout the day.
- Follow a low-fat diet and avoid overeating to limit the risk of obesity.
- Limit alcohol consumption as this affects blood sugar control.
- Limit caffeine intake as coffee, tea and fizzy drinks affect sugar control.
- Choose green tea instead of your normal brew for its antioxidant catechins which support pancreatic function.
- Add herbs and spices such as cinnamon to your food to improve glucose metabolism and blood sugar control.

| Stick to... | Stay away from... |
| --- | --- |
| Low-GI foods. | High-GI foods. |
| High-fibre foods. | Sweets and chocolate. |
| Green tea. | Refined carbohydrates. |
| Protein at each meal. | Alcohol. |
| Cinnamon and other anti-hyperglycaemic herbs and spices. | Coffee, tea and cola. |
| | Too many starchy carbohydrates. |

# Chapter Four

# Food for Thought

Although we automatically reach for food and drink to cheer us up, improve concentration, or even help us get to sleep, not many people make the connection between mental function and their diet, yet the two are closely linked. Why do you drink milk to help you sleep and coffee to perk you up? Why does chocolate cheer you up? Does fish really make you brainy?

According to the NHS, 1 in 4 of us will experience a mental health condition at some point (NHS, 2010), and an increasing amount of research is being done illustrating vital links between fatty acid deficiency and impaired cognitive (mental) function. Conditions such as dementia, ADHD, depression, anxiety, dyslexia and other mental health conditions often respond well to fatty acid supplementation and an improved diet.

We all have ups and downs, but whether your mood swings are passing or long term, there may be several dietary adjustments that can help.

## Premenstrual syndrome

Premenstrual syndrome (PMS) is the name given to describe symptoms such as fluid retention, irritability, mood swings and breast tenderness experienced in the two weeks before a woman's monthly period. The exact cause of PMS is not fully understood but it is thought to be linked to changing hormone levels, and there are several dietary factors that have been linked to PMS.

## Low blood sugar

Low blood sugar and cravings for sweet foods and refined carbohydrates are common at this time of the month, as changing hormone levels affect insulin production, which in turn affects blood sugar levels.

You can help to stabilise blood sugar levels by:

- Eating slow-release, low-GI carbohydrates such as oats and beans.

- Avoiding or reducing stimulants such as caffeine, alcohol and nicotine.

- Reducing high-GI, quick-release carbohydrates such as sugary foods.

- Eating at least three meals daily with snacks in between.

- Filling up on wholesome foods such as beans and pulses, vegetables, rice, oats, nuts, seeds, fish and lean meats rich in the nutrients which help to control blood sugar levels.

## Chocolate

'A small bar of dark chocolate can contain more caffeine than a cup of instant coffee, so imagine the combined effects of coffee and chocolate!'

Chocolate is the food we choose to lift our mood, and chocolate craving is even listed as a symptom of PMS and seasonal affective disorder. There are several ingredients in chocolate that contribute to craving, mild addiction and mood improvement.

- Firstly, the sugar in chocolate elevates our blood sugar levels, and caffeine in chocolate stimulates the conversion of stored carbohydrates into glucose (sugar), elevating our blood sugar levels even further.

- Secondly, the elevated sugar levels stimulate insulin production, and this in turn increases the absorption of an amino acid called tryptophan. Tryptophan is taken up by brain cells and converted into serotonin, the feel-good hormone.

- Thirdly, chocolate also contains a variety of other compounds including: theobromine, which acts alongside caffeine as a stimulant, anandamides, which have a subtle cannabis-like effect on the brain, and substances such as phenylethylamine, which is produced naturally in the brain and released at times of emotional arousal.

Dark and milk chocolate both have the ability to affect mental function due to the combination of the stimulants caffeine and theobromine.

Dark chocolate (also known as plain chocolate) has even been heralded by some as a 'superfood' due to its antioxidant content. One study (Lee *et al.*, 2003) found higher levels of antioxidants in dark chocolate than in red wine and green tea, and separate studies on cocoa (the active ingredient of chocolate) have illustrated a blood pressure-lowering effect.

| | White chocolate | Milk chocolate | Dark (plain) chocolate |
|---|---|---|---|
| Magnesium | 26 | 50 | 89 |
| Iron | 0.2 | 1.4 | 2.3 |
| Zinc | 0.9 | 1.1 | 1.3 |
| Manganese | 0.02 | 0.22 | 0.63 |

All values are mg per 100g.

(Source: statistics are sourced from Food Standards Agency, 2002. © Crown Copyright.)

So it's not all bad news for chocolate, but if you're going to indulge, use it as an occasional treat and it will do more to lift your mood than if you eat it every day – as with all stimulants. There is a significant difference in nutrient levels when dark, milk and white chocolate are compared, so choose dark chocolate to benefit from the extra antioxidants and minerals, and maybe a little of what you fancy really will do you good!

## Serotonin

Levels of feel-good hormones called endorphins drop prior to menstruation, which can cause nausea, moodiness and increased agitation. In particular, serotonin levels decrease, affecting mood and increasing sensitivity to pain.

Serotonin is a neurotransmitter, enabling chemical messages to travel around our brain. Serotonin is formed from tryptophan, which is an essential amino acid found in protein foods. The insulin released when we eat carbohydrate foods has the same effect chocolate has – it increases the amount of tryptophan taken up by the brain cells, enabling more serotonin formation, thus boosting our mood and helping us to relax. This is why a happy, relaxed feeling is sometimes experienced after a big plate of pasta or bread. So, eating carbohydrate foods with tryptophan-rich foods will boost your mood even more. Serotonin also initiates sleep.

Tryptophan-rich foods include:

- Turkey.
- Chicken.
- Avocados.
- Bananas.
- Broccoli.
- Spinach.

## Fatty acid imbalance

Pain and tenderness during PMS may also be increased by an imbalance in hormone-like substances called prostaglandins. Prostaglandins are dependent upon the correct balance of essential fatty acids, so a deficiency of either omega 3 fatty acids or any of the nutrients which enable conversion of omega 6 fatty acids into anti-inflammatory prostaglandins may result in inflammation or increased blood clotting.

Many women take evening primrose oil. This is rich in a fatty acid called gamma linolenic acid, which enables formation of both pro-inflammatory and anti-inflammatory prostaglandins. Taking gamma linolenic acid may help to rebalance the competition between pro-imflammatory and anti-inflammatory fatty acids, with the result of reducing inflammation and blood clotting.

Although harmless and effective for some, taking evening primrose oil is creating a short cut to aid balanced prostaglandin formation rather than correcting a potential fatty acid imbalance. Some evening primrose oil supplements are combined with fatty acid or fish oils, which will help to rebalance pro-inflammatory and anti-inflammatory pathways. However, if you suffer with abdominal cramps, breast tenderness, headaches, constipation or diarrhoea, you may benefit from these dietary adjustments:

- Swap meat for fish.

- Snack on linseeds and walnuts instead of crisps and sweets.

- Use linseed oil or rapeseed oil for salad dressings.

- Cook with olive oil instead of safflower or sunflower oils.

## Vitamin and mineral levels

Low levels of zinc, magnesium, vitamin B6 and vitamin E have all been connected with PMS, so following a healthy, varied diet is important. A multi-vitamin, multi-mineral supplement will help you to correct deficiencies, although mineral deficiencies in particular may take a number of months to correct.

### Zinc imbalance

Zinc supplementation prior to menstruation has proved successful in some women, possibly due to low zinc levels and its interaction in the inflammatory prostaglandin pathways which control inflammation and pain. Simply ensuring that you consume plenty of zinc in your diet may be all you need to do to improve PMS symptoms, or consider a zinc-rich, multi-vitamin multi-mineral.

Certain lifestyle factors can increase our need for zinc – if any of the following apply to you, you may need more zinc in your diet.

- Long-term use of the contraceptive pill.

- Smoking.

- Alcohol consumption.

- Chronic stress.

Zinc-rich foods include oysters, wholegrains, pumpkin seeds, meat and offal. Zinc-rich foods tend to be of animal or seafood origin, so vegetarian and vegan diets need to ensure a good intake of wholegrains and pumpkin seeds.

## Magnesium

Magnesium levels can be low during PMS, which may be a reason for the common 'chocolate cravings' experienced at this time of the month. Trials have shown significantly improved mood changes in women taking magnesium supplements. Try eating more of these foods throughout the month, and remember that it may take a number of months to increase your magnesium levels before you notice a difference:

- Cauliflower.
- Bananas.
- Pumpkin.
- Brown rice.
- Nuts.
- Seeds.

## Iron

Iron levels are also likely to be low during and immediately after menstruation, causing an increased requirement and potential craving for foods rich in this mineral, such as red meat, seafood or eggs.

## Vitamin B6

Vitamin B6 is commonly used to help reduce the symptoms of PMS, and seems to be particularly helpful for mood swings.

Some ideas to increase your vitamin B6 intake could include:

- Add a seed mix to fortified cereals.
- Enjoy trout poached with vegetables.
- Add grilled strips of meat to stir-fries.

## An anti-PMS diet

Follow these tips in the week prior to your period and try out the seven-day eating plan for PMS in chapter 7.

- Eat low-GI carbohydrates (see page 50) to help control blood sugar levels.

- Choose unrefined wholegrains to increase your intake of essential nutrients such as zinc.

- Eat small amounts of protein at each meal to help slow down the release of glucose into the bloodstream – this will help to stabilise blood sugar levels, and the protein also provides vitamin B6 and zinc.

- Swap meat for fish to increase fatty acid intake that will boost anti-inflammatory pathways and reduce swelling and pain. Alternatively, introduce linseeds, linseed oil and walnuts into your diet as these all provide linolenic acid which helps to reduce inflammatory reactions.

# Depression and seasonal affective disorder

A depressed mood ranges from feeling low or having temporary conditions such as seasonal affective disorder (SAD), to long-term depression. With such a wide range of causes, symptoms and conditions, it is impossible to address them all individually here. However, there are a number of dietary elements that commonly affect our mood, so adjusting your diet as follows is a good place to start.

'There are significant correlations between worldwide fish consumption and rates of depression.'

## Fatty acids

Clinically depressed people often have lower levels of omega 3 fatty acids in their blood, and several studies have shown that supplementing a diet with omega 3 fatty acids can improve depression. Eating more omega 3 fatty acids leads to a higher volume of grey matter in the areas of the brain associated with emotional arousal and regulation, and these fats also enhance mood. Higher consumption of seafood in some countries has been linked with protection against depression, bipolar disorder and SAD.

# B vitamins

Symptoms affecting the brain and mental function have been linked with a number of the B vitamins. Relatively low levels of each of the B vitamins are required to maintain good health and these are found in a wide range of foods, usually occurring together. If you make sure you base each meal around these foods, it is unlikely you will have a deficiency of B vitamins:

- Vegetables.

- Wholegrains.

- Fruit.

- Beans and pulses.

- Eggs.

- Meat.

- Fish.

- Dairy produce.

Vitamin B1 (also known as thiamine) mimics and maximises the action of an important neurotransmitter involved in memory function called acetyl choline. In several double-blind, placebo controlled studies, thiamine supplementation improved mood and feelings of wellbeing, with participants also reporting increased clear-headedness and faster reaction times. To increase your intake of vitamin B1, try the following:

- Add a seed mix to fortified cereals.

- For a quick snack, eat beans on wholemeal toast.

- Enjoy mixed beans in chillies, curries and casseroles.

A number of studies have reported an association between deficiencies of folic acid or vitamin B12 and psychiatric conditions such as dementia and depression. For more vitamin B12 try:

- A breakfast of eggs on toast.

- Adding tofu to stir-fries.

- Eating yoghurt for a healthy snack.

# Folic acid

A high percentage of depressed patients have been found to have poor folic acid levels. Folic acid is involved in producing neurotransmitters, and without ample levels of neurotransmitters our mental function quickly becomes impaired. For more folic acid in your diet:

- Eat raspberries with fortified breakfast cereals.
- Always add spinach, rocket or watercress to salad sandwiches.
- Enjoy salads with salmon or cottage cheese.

# Vitamin D

It's funny how a spell in the sunshine makes us feel happier and the winter months can lower mood; in those of us more susceptible to the change in seasons, this is diagnosed as seasonal affective disorder. But it's possible we are right to trust our mood, as we create most of our vitamin D in sunlight, and several large-scale studies have reported that vitamin D supplementation has an anti-depressant effect, with some researchers stating that depression increases when vitamin D levels dip below normal. Although vitamin D is found in eggs, dairy foods, oily fish, fortified margarines and cereals, a little sunlight really boosts vitamin D production.

# Zinc

Several studies have linked psychological symptoms to low zinc levels; in one study of 174 older adults, 71% of subjects with zinc deficiency displayed a higher value on a depression test against 29% of subjects with a normal zinc value (Marcellini *et al.*, 2006). Common symptoms of zinc deficiency include the following:

- White specks on nails.
- Stretch marks in the skin.
- Poor blood sugar control.
- Mood swings and depression.

# ADHD, hyperactivity, dyslexia and autism

Although these are all separate conditions, their occurrence often overlaps in families and in individuals, the conditions share many symptoms and they often respond well to the same dietary adjustments. In particular, scientific evidence suggests that fatty acid deficiencies or imbalances may contribute to a wide range of behavioural and learning disorders.

## Fatty acids

Essential fatty acids and long-chain fatty acids are often lacking in our diet, and a high intake of saturated and refined fats and even omega 6 fatty acids worsens our fatty acid balance even more. Research shows positive results in hyperactivity, antisocial behaviour and cognitive function following fatty acid supplementation, especially where a combination of long-chain omega 3 fatty acids and gamma linolenic acid are taken together.

## Whole foods vs junk foods

A diet full of processed foods is lacking in the nutrients that we need to feed our brain, resulting in symptoms such as irritability, aggression, inability to concentrate and depression. In addition to being devoid of minerals and vitamins, added sugar also creates fluctuations in blood sugar levels, contributing to hyperactivity, mood swings and poor concentration.

## Additives

In 2007, *The Food Magazine* reported that several colourings and preservatives regularly used in food and drinks have to carry health warnings regarding allergic and hyperactivity reactions if they are added to medicines – yet don't have to carry such warnings on foods and drinks. These additives are commonly used in products such as cakes, sweets and soft drinks.

Many additives are outlawed in other countries including the US and Japan, but are still added to cheap, processed foods available in the UK. This is despite studies reporting that the behaviour of hyperactive children improves when artificial food colourings are excluded from their diet. However, an EU-wide health warning must now be put on any food or drink that contains the following artificial colourings thought to cause hyperactivity in children:

- Tartrazine (E102).
- Sunset yellow (E110).
- Quinoline Yellow (E104).
- Carmoisine (E122).
- Ponceau Red (E124).
- Allura Red (E129).

You should also watch out for preservatives such as sodium benzoate, sodium dioxide and sodium metabisulphite.

The average improvement from eliminating these additives from the diet is around one third to one half of the improvement typically associated with medication for ADHD.

Not all additives are bad – some E numbers are natural compounds that are actually good for you. Check out the full list of E numbers at www.ukfoodguide. net/enumeric to see what you need to avoid.

For improved focus and attention try to:

- Avoid foods with artificial additives and a long list of E numbers.
- Stabilise blood sugar levels to avoid low blood sugar, hyperactivity (from high blood sugar) and lack of concentration by introducing slow-release carbohydrates such as porridge and beans into the diet.
- Include protein foods such as eggs, fish or meat in each meal to slow down glucose release into the bloodstream.
- Eat fish or vegetable sources of linolenic acid (linseeds, walnuts) to provide a good source of long-chain fatty acids for the brain.

'Research with school children has shown improvements in attention, problem solving and memory when comparing the effect of breakfast versus no breakfast.'

# A menu to maximise mental performance

Try eating some of the meals listed in this menu to improve your cognitive function.

## Breakfasts

Milky porridge with added mixed seeds, chopped walnuts and fruit.

Omega 3 fortified boiled egg with toasted wholemeal bread.

Scrambled/poached egg (fortified) on wholemeal toast with baked beans.

## Lunches

Tuna or salmon salad sandwich with wholemeal bread.

Corn tortilla wrap with turkey, spinach, bean sprouts and avocado.

Sardines on wholemeal toast.

## Dinners

Turkey or salmon risotto.

Vegetable chilli with brown rice.

Good quality fish fingers or homemade fish cakes with baked beans or peas and roasted jacket potato skins.

## Snacks

Piece of fruit.

Nut or seed mix.

Nut or seed bar.

Oat cereal bar with no added sugar.

# Cognitive function

As we age, our cognitive function is directly linked with our nutritional status. In short, a healthy diet sustains a healthy mind. In the same way that free radicals create cell damage in other parts of the body such as oxidising cholesterol (see page 9), the same oxidative damage occurs in the brain cells. Dementia is usually a result of several degenerative changes in the brain over a period of time.

Our brains contain large amounts of fatty tissue – the reason for the old wives tale 'fish makes you brainy' is that the long-chain fatty acids found in fish form much of the structure of the brain. However, these long-chain fatty acids are polyunsaturated, meaning that these fatty acids are at greater risk of oxidative damage, as a polyunsaturated fat has lots of 'gaps' in its structure where oxygen can attach.

Prevention of oxidative damage is better than cure, so following a few simple dietary tips to maintain good mental health can go some way to helping prevent damage.

▪ Eat fish regularly (or take an omega 3 supplement).

▪ Include antioxidants to protect the long-chain fatty acids.

## A menu rich in long-chain fatty acids and antioxidants

### Breakfasts

Kedgeree – smoked mackerel with brown rice and wilted spinach – with a glass of orange or red grape juice.

### Lunches

Peppered mackerel with a green leafy salad, beetroot, tomatoes, red onion and grated carrot.

## Dinners

Tuna steak with olive oil roasted squash, sweet potato and carrots, served with broccoli.

## Snacks

Walnuts and linseeds with cranberries or acai berries.

Pieces of cooked or smoked fish with avocado, beetroot, peppers and carrots.

Seed and nut mix with walnuts and linseeds and a glass of fresh fruit juice.

Cereal with added walnuts, linseeds, berries, mango, kiwi and red grapes.

# Alzheimer's disease

Alzheimer's disease is thought to be caused by plaques and tangles developing in the brain, in conjunction with oxidative damage which causes brain cell degeneration and mental ageing. There is also thought to be a genetic factor involved, but a number of nutritional elements have illustrated a significant effect upon the occurrence and severity of Alzheimer's disease.

## Fish

Research has repeatedly shown improvements in memory and cognitive performance following consumption of more omega 3 fatty acids found in fish or fish oil supplements.

- The brain contains a high proportion of fatty tissue, of which 65% is made up of the same long-chain fatty acids found in fish – eicosapentaenoic acid (EPA) and docosahexaenoic acid (DHA), as covered in chapter 2 (see page 36).

- DHA is found in the structure of the brain, whereas EPA improves blood flow to the brain, also boosting brain function and acting as a natural anti-inflammatory. These fatty acids are essential for normal brain development and function.

- These fatty acids form part of the nerve sheath that surrounds the nerve cells, maintaining membrane flexibility and providing essential insulation for electrical signals to pass from one nerve cell to another, creating our thought processes.

Non-fish eaters could take a fish or krill oil supplement or get fatty acids from nuts and seeds. Walnuts and linseeds contain fats that can be converted into long-chain fatty acids in the body; however, the conversion rates from 'non-fish' fatty acids are very low. Conversion is affected badly by a diet high in saturated fats or too many omega 6 fatty acids, so if you are relying on non-fish sources of fatty acids, you should:

- Reduce your intake of saturated fats found in meats, eggs and dairy produce.

- Avoid refined (trans and hydrogenated) fats.

- Limit safflower or sunflower vegetable oils as these contain more omega 6 fats which will reduce conversion of omega 3 fats into the long-chain fatty acids found in fish.

- Use linseed or rapeseed oils for salad dressings as these contain more omega 3 fats and less omega 6 fats.

- Use olive oil for cooking – it's not particularly rich in omega 3 fats, but it contains considerably less omega 6 fats than most other oils, and is less prone to oxidation than rapeseed or linseed oils.

'Tinned fish loses much of its natural oil during the canning process, so fish such as tinned tuna and salmon will only contain approximately the same amount of omega 3 oils as fresh white fish.'

| Good sources of omega 3 fats | Non-fish options |
| --- | --- |
| Sardines | Linseeds or linseed oil |
| Salmon | Walnuts |
| Trout | fortified orange juice |
| Herring | Omega 3 fortified eggs |
| Tuna | Omega 3 fortified yoghurt |
| Pilchards | Green leafy vegetables |

The fats found in the non-fish sources listed above are not rich in EPA or DHA, but they offer the shorter-chain fatty acid (alpha linolenic acid) which the body can convert into the long-chain EPA or DHA used in the brain.

The table below shows which fresh fish count as oily and which are non-oily. Oily fish contain higher amounts of the long-chain fatty acids EPA and DHA, non-oily fish contain these oils too but just not as much.

| Oily fish | White/non-oily fish |
|-----------|---------------------|
| Salmon | Cod |
| Mackerel | Haddock |
| Trout | Coley |
| Herring | Plaice |
| Sardines | Lemon sole |
| Pilchards | Whiting |
| Tuna | Halibut |
| Swordfish | Skate |
| Kipper | Rock salmon |
| Anchovies | Dover sole |

'To consume enough EPA and DHA, eat between one to two portions of fish each week (or up to four portions as long as you are not pregnant or breastfeeding), and make half of the fish you eat oily fish.'

## How much EPA or DHA do we need?

The Food Standards Agency recommends eating between two to four portions of fish a week, half of which should be oily fish. This provides approximately 450mg of omega 3 fatty acids every day; 500mg per day is generally accepted as a healthy intake. However, some people respond well to intakes of 1,000mg or more daily, particularly those suffering with health conditions such as:

- Dementia.
- ADHD.
- Depression.
- Anxiety.
- Autism.
- Dyslexia.

80

If you suffer with any of these health conditions and think you may benefit from more fatty acids, the first step is to adjust your diet so that you are consuming more essential fatty acids.

## Omega 3-rich meal ideas

### Breakfasts

Kippers and omega 3-enriched orange juice.

Kedgeree.

Omega 3 fortified egg on wholemeal toast.

### Lunches

Fresh (or tinned) sardines with a large, green leafy salad, cherry tomatoes, beetroot and carrot.

Jacket potato with tuna or salmon and salad vegetables.

### Dinners

Salmon with broccoli, sweet potato and carrots.

Tuna steak with roasted squash, carrots and broccoli.

Spinach and sweet potato risotto drizzled with omega 3 oil.

### Snacks

Nut or seed bars containing linseeds or flaxseeds.

A handful of walnuts.

Omega 3 fortified yoghurt (dairy or soya) with added walnuts and linseeds.

DHA has been shown to be deficient in the brains of Alzheimer's patients when compared with healthy individuals of the same age, and preliminary studies indicate that low blood levels of DHA is a significant risk factor for the development of Alzheimer's and reduced cognitive function. As fish is rich in DHA, it makes sense to include it in our diet.

# Fruit and vegetables

Foods rich in antioxidants may help to prevent oxidative damage occurring, hence reducing the risk of conditions such as Alzheimer's. Some foods are particularly rich in plant nutrients with powerful therapeutic properties. In one study of 1,836 adults (Dai *et al.*, 2006), there was a reduced incidence in those who drank juices at least three times per week compared with those who drank certain types of juice less often than once per week. This was thought to be due to the plant nutrient content of fruit and vegetable juices.

'Drink unsweetened red grape juice or cranberry juice every day.'

## Eat a rainbow diet

Different coloured foods contain different nutrients. Eat a rainbow diet for maximum impact on all neurological disorders – follow the diet for mood and cognitive function in chapter 7 or gain inspiration from *What Colour Is Your Diet?* by David Heber.

| Purple/red | Plums, purple grapes, strawberries, blueberries, blackberries. |
|---|---|
| Red | Tomatoes, water melon, pink grapefruit. |
| Orange | Squash, carrots, sweet potato, pumpkin, cantaloupe melon. |
| Orange/yellow | Peaches, papaya, oranges, nectarines, apricots, tangerines. |
| Dark green | Cabbage, broccoli, sprouts, kale, rocket, watercress. |
| Green/yellow | Avocado, honeydew melon, peas, sweetcorn, spinach. |
| Green/white | Garlic, onions, shallots, celery, pears, chicory, chives. |

## Zinc

Zinc deficiency is widespread and becomes increasingly common as we age. It is required for many antioxidant enzymes, so a deficiency may result in higher levels of cellular damage, including oxidative damage to brain cells. Zinc levels in the brains of those suffering with Alzheimer's disease are often found to be considerably lower, and it has been suggested that zinc deficiency may be a significant causative factor. Supplementation of this mineral in Alzheimer's patients has yielded unbelievable results in some patients, with significant improvements in up to 80% of patients in some studies.

Some ideas to increase your daily zinc intake could include:

- Adding pumpkin seeds and wheat germ to cereals and yoghurts.

- Eating shellfish regularly and enjoying oysters when eating out.

- Eating dark cuts of meat (leg rather than breast) as they contain more zinc.

## The aluminium theory

Although there is no conclusive proof that aluminium causes Alzheimer's disease, it has been proven that as we age, blood aluminium levels increase, and those suffering with Alzheimer's disease have significantly higher levels of aluminium in their brains than normal. The most effective way to avoid this is to limit your intake of aluminium:

- Don't use aluminium pots and pans.

- Avoid using aluminium foil to wrap food.

- Choose anti-perspirants that don't contain aluminium.

- Avoid the use of antacids for heartburn.

- Although aluminium occurs naturally in water, some water companies add it as a water treatment, so it may be worth checking with your local supplier or swapping to bottled water.

- Use a water filter jug to filter out aluminium.

- Don't add salt to food as aluminium is sometimes added to table salt.

# Herbs and spices to help mental function

There are some herbs that are often linked with improvements in mental and emotional conditions.

## Gingko biloba

Gingko biloba has been used as a medicinal herb for thousands of years, often used to improve memory and to help reduce the symptoms of dementia. It works by widening the arteries in the brain and improving blood circulation to the brain. Gingko biloba contains several different active compounds including antioxidant plant nutrients which help to counteract oxidative damage.

Gingko biloba has been known to enhance memory, learning, intellect and emotion.

## St John's wort

Another herb used to improve mental function is St John's wort, which has several medicinal uses but is commonly taken to reduce insomnia and depression. It is thought to work by increasing the concentration or effectiveness of serotonin in the brain, enhancing a feeling of wellbeing. As with most supplements, you should check with your doctor or qualified nutritional practitioner before taking St John's Wart, as it can interfere with the effectiveness of other medications you may be taking.

## Phosphatidyl serine

This nutrient determines the fluidity and function of cell membranes in the brain. The richest source in the diet is soya, but food does not provide enough of this nutrient, and a healthy body usually manufactures what it needs. However, if we lack essential fatty acids, folic acid or vitamin B12 in the diet, our ability to manufacture phosphatidyl serine is affected. With advancing age we seem to become less able to form this nutrient, and low levels are specifically associated with impaired mental function and dementia.

Although supplementation with this nutrient may be useful, the first steps are to ensure a diet rich in the nutrients we need to naturally manufacture phosphatidyl serine in the body – so fill up on these foods and see if it makes a difference to your memory!

- Eat fish, walnuts and linseeds or nut and seed oils (especially linseed oil) for the essential fatty acids you've already read so much about.

- Folic acid is found in foods such as raspberries, green leafy vegetables, beans, salmon, cottage cheese and fortified breakfast cereals.

- Vitamin B12 can be found in eggs, meat, fish, dairy foods, tofu and fortified cereals.

# Not a fish fan?

If fish isn't your idea of a tasty meal or snack, you may benefit from supplementing with fish oils. Look for a supplement that provides 500mg to 1,000mg (1g) of EPA and DHA.

# Important note

Many nutrients are involved in healthy mental function, and several antioxidant vitamins and minerals are needed to help prevent oxidative damage that can lead to brain cell degeneration. Therefore, rather than supplement with any one nutrient, it is recommended that unless you are following a treatment plan prescribed by a qualified practitioner, a multi-vitamin, multi-mineral supplement is the best way to increase nutrient intake alongside a healthy diet.

In most cases of mental impairment, best results following nutrient supplementation are observed when symptoms have been present for less than six months. When symptoms have been present for longer, it takes more time to correct nutrient deficiencies or imbalances, and in some cases the deficiencies may never fully recover, particularly in dementia and Alzheimer's disease.

Even better than correcting deficiencies swiftly is preventing them in the first place: prevention is always better than cure.

# Summing Up

Feed your brain what it needs!

- Eat fish two to four times weekly for the long-chain fatty acids known to benefit cognitive function.

- Include foods rich in plant-based omega 3 fatty acids in your diet, such as linseeds, linseed oil, walnuts and green leafy vegetables. This is especially important if you don't eat fish.

- Make sure you eat at least five servings of fresh fruit and vegetables daily to maximise your antioxidant intake and help prevent oxidative damage to brain cells.

- Consume fruits and vegetables rich in polyphenols, anthocyanidins and antioxidants, in particular berries, red grapes and cherries.

- Include tryptophan-rich foods in your diet (turkey, chicken, avocado, banana, broccoli and spinach) to maximise formation of the feel good hormone serotonin.

- Avoid or limit stimulants such as coffee, tea, alcohol and sugar – in the long term, these are detrimental to blood glucose regulation and can cause hyperactivity and behavioural difficulties. They may lift mood temporarily but are not a long-term fix.

- Drink antioxidant green tea to limit free radical damage to brain cells.

- Try to eliminate all sources of aluminium in your diet.

- Eat a zinc-rich diet – fill up on wholegrains, pumpkin seeds, seafood and lean cuts of meat.

- Eat regularly to maintain a constant source of energy for the brain.

- Get a little sunshine to boost vitamin D production.

- If your diet is already good, supplementing with omega 3 fatty acids or other nutrients may help. You are advised to seek the help of a qualified practitioner for the best supplement prescription to suit you.

| Stick to... | Stay away from... |
|---|---|
| Fish and omega 3 fortified foods. | Refined carbohydrates and sugar. |
| Linseeds and walnuts. | Alcohol. |
| Green leafy vegetables. | Coffee, tea and cola. |
| Green tea. | |
| A rainbow coloured diet for antioxidants and phytonutrients. | |
| Tryptophan-rich foods (turkey, chicken, avocado, banana, broccoli and spinach). | |
| Zinc-rich foods (wholegrains, pumpkin seeds, seafood and lean cuts of meat). | |

# Chapter Five

# Healthy Tums

Digestive complaints are one of the most common reasons for consulting a GP or nutritionist, and colon cancer is the third most common cancer in men and the second most common cancer in women, yet it is largely avoidable. Irritable bowel syndrome (IBS) affects 15-20% of the population in Westernised societies, and over-the-counter remedies for heartburn and indigestion are amongst the most commonly used medications. Heartburn, indigestion and IBS can all be avoided, controlled or improved through diet – which makes sense when you consider it is usually our diet causing these problems in the first place!

## Conditions affecting the digestive tract

### Indigestion

Where indigestion is referred to as acid indigestion, this is usually the same as heartburn, but the term indigestion covers a range of symptoms including discomfort or bloating in the stomach or intestinal area.

### Heartburn and acid reflux

Heartburn is usually caused by an excess of acid in the stomach, often rising up into the oesophagus (acid reflux), creating a burning feeling. We secrete hydrochloric acid into the stomach whenever we digest foods or drinks, but various problems can occur:

■ Some people create too much acid.

'Food is not classed as being in the body until it has been absorbed through the gut wall... the digestive tract creates a barrier between the exterior environment and the inside of the body.'

- Some do not create excess acid, but the stomach wall may be affected by the acid if, for example, stomach ulcers have occurred.

- Some people experience indigestion if they fail to secrete enough acid.

- The lower oesophageal sphincter muscle, which usually stops acidic stomach contents from rising up the oesophagus from the stomach, may be faulty.

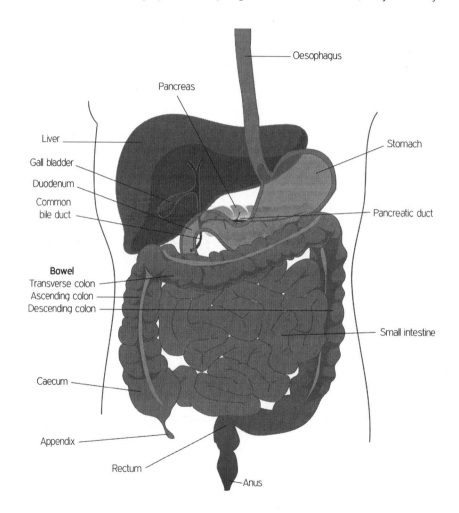

# Undigested food

Apart from fibre which passes through the gut largely undigested, all other food nutrients should be digested (broken down into smaller particles) and absorbed by the time they reach the end of the small intestine. However, in some circumstances undigested food may be seen in the stools. This can be as a result of:

- Food not being chewed well enough, leaving it too large for enzymes to completely break down.

- Food passing through the gut too quickly to be thoroughly digested.

- Lack of digestive enzymes which normally break food down.

- Lack of other nutrients required for digestion and absorption.

If food is not being thoroughly digested and absorbed into the body, you will not be getting the nutrients and energy that you require. Undigested food in the colon encourages 'bad' bacteria to accumulate, causing gas and putrefactive substances that alter the bowel flora (the type of bacteria in your bowel) and cause symptoms such as flatulence.

You may be able to recognise undigested foods in your stools, which can help you to figure out which type of foods you are having trouble digesting. For example:

- Meat in the stools indicates you are not breaking down proteins.

- A pale coloured stool indicates poor fat digestion.

- Undigested cereal or vegetables indicates undigested carbohydrates, though remember that fibre such as tomato or pepper skins and sweetcorn normally remain largely undigested.

# Gall bladder removed

The gall bladder stores and squirts bile into the small intestine to help digest fats. Bile is made by the liver, so when the gall bladder is removed, bile still travels down the common bile duct into the small intestine, but it is less concentrated and is a continuous trickle rather than a squirt when it is needed (when fats enter the small intestine). So if you have had your gall bladder removed, you may struggle to digest fats properly, and experience indigestion and fatty (pale) stools.

## IBS

IBS is a term used to describe a combination of gastro-intestinal symptoms such as abdominal bloating and pain, flatulence, diarrhoea and constipation, and 'dumping syndrome', when the bowel empties involuntarily. It is often worse when the individual is stressed, and can be caused or worsened by eating certain foods. Key factors usually include problems with digestion and absorption of foods, gut motility and bowel flora imbalances.

## Leaky gut syndrome

'IBS is a popular medical diagnosis often reached once everything else has been excluded.'

If anything irritates our gut lining, the intestinal wall can become more porous – this is known as leaky gut syndrome. Larger gaps in the intestinal wall allow bigger particles to move into the intestinal wall, often creating allergic responses as the immune system attacks these larger molecules which have not yet been fully digested. This also means that as food has not been fully broken down, you will not benefit from all the nutrients that the food has to offer.

## Diarrhoea

If the bowel is irritated by microbial infection, caffeine or other consumables, it can contract and empty the contents before the large intestine has had chance to reabsorb sufficient water – the result is diarrhoea.

## Constipation

Although it is healthy to empty the bowel at least daily, many people in the Western world empty the bowel less frequently. Contraction of the bowel walls is controlled by the nervous system – in balance, different branches of the nervous system enable the gut to relax and contract as necessary, but factors such as stress can unbalance the nervous system and result in a tight, over-contracted bowel. Dietary factors which contribute to constipation include:

- Inadequate fluid intake.
- Inadequate fibre intake.

Regular diarrhoea, constipation or inability to form and pass healthy stools may also be an indication of unbalanced bowel flora and unfavourable bowel environment, known as dysbiosis.

# Change your diet to suit your gut

There are some dietary changes that will help to alleviate a specific condition, but many recommendations will help more than one part of the gastro-intestinal tract. These changes sometimes involve removing foods from your diet that you may be intolerant of. Food sensitivity, intolerance or allergy can affect all parts of the digestive tract from the mouth through to the anus, so removing allergens may benefit the entire digestive system, and even beneficially affect other areas of the body such as the skin, mood and immune system.

# Heartburn

There are several foods and drinks to initially avoid which may cause heartburn – either through intolerance or because of increased sensitivity in the gastro-intestinal tract. Foods and drinks to avoid include:

- Tea and coffee.
- Alcohol.
- Spicy foods.
- Wheat.
- Dairy foods.
- Citrus foods.
- Eggs.
- Refined carbohydrates and foods with a high sugar content.
- Fatty foods.
- Too much protein.

## Fatty foods

Although fats do not begin to be digested until they reach your small intestine, they often cause heartburn sufferers problems while in the stomach. Fatty meats, cheese, cream and other full-fat dairy produce, chocolate and desserts should be avoided or at least limited until the foods that are causing or worsening the heartburn have been found.

'Although it's best to figure out which foods may be causing your heartburn and cut them out of your diet, simply avoiding lying down for a couple of hours after eating, or raising the head end of your bed can help to stop acid reflux.'

## Too much protein

Although we produce acid in the stomach to kill bacteria in all types of food, we produce more acid to digest protein foods. So if your diet is high in protein, this may cause excessive acid secretion. In this case, the following foods should be limited:

- Meat.
- Fish.
- Eggs.
- Dairy produce.
- Soya products.

## Will antacid remedies help?

Antacids either neutralise stomach acid or reduce your secretion of acid in the stomach – both may alleviate your symptoms but do not help your digestion!

Often, gastro-intestinal secretions and function will return to normal once a food or substance that is upsetting the inner lining of the gut is removed. For heartburn, it may be enough to simply reduce the amount of the food culprit(s) causing problems, but sometimes it has to be removed completely. The only way to know what is causing the problem is to exclude typical or suspected foods from your diet, keep a check on your symptoms and then re-introduce excluded foods one at a time until you can identify the food(s) causing problems.

## Too little acid

You may not be producing enough acid in the stomach, which can also cause indigestion as protein foods are not being broken down. This may create problems in the bowel as undigested proteins upset the healthy bowel environment. Although protein foods stimulate greater gastric secretion, eating more protein at this stage is not recommended, as until you are adequately digesting proteins, eating more will not help. Therefore, a low protein therapeutic diet to help normalise digestive function is recommended alongside the temporary use of gastric acid and digestive enzyme supplements. An exclusion diet eliminating foods causing digestive problems may also help.

## Food and drinks that may help to alleviate heartburn

- Chamomile, peppermint, fennel or ginger tea – they all have various anti-spasmodic and anti-inflammatory properties.

- Onions – although they can cause indigestion for some, they possess anti-inflammatory properties, so should be included in the diet if they can be eaten.

- Turmeric – this has anti-inflammatory properties. While this spice is usually added to curries and other spicy meals which may not be easily tolerated, supplements containing the active ingredient curcumin are available.

- Ginger – this will improve digestion as it activates production of saliva, gastric juice and bile, and improves gut motility.

# Undigested food

The first thing to do is to make sure you are chewing your food adequately so that it is broken down into small enough particles to be digested. If food is passing through the gut too quickly to be thoroughly digested, this suggests that the gut wall may be irritated in places, and you may benefit from eliminating suspect foods in order for the gut wall to mend and enable digestion to return to normal.

If the pancreas or sections of the gut wall are dysfunctional then you may not be secreting sufficient amounts of digestive enzymes to digest your food. You would need to consult your GP or a qualified nutritional practitioner to help identify if, and why, you are lacking digestive enzymes. Taking digestive enzymes can help with this condition in the short term, but ideally your GP or nutritional practitioner will work towards normalising digestive function.

## No gall bladder

If you have had your gall bladder removed, you may find it helpful to reduce fats and fatty foods in your diet, particularly:

- Cream and creamy foods.
- Ice cream.
- Full-fat yoghurts.
- Cheese, butter and margarine.
- Oils.
- Fatty meats.
- Vegetable foods with a high-fat content such as nuts, seeds and avocado.

# IBS

IBS is often caused by one or more substances irritating the inside of the gut wall. Once the gut wall is irritated, other foods which may previously have been tolerated might also cause problems. Therefore, most nutritional therapists will usually suggest an exclusion diet to identify and eradicate the food or drink culprits causing the problem. Here are some foods that are commonly excluded:

- Wheat.
- Dairy foods.
- Citrus foods.
- Eggs.

- Chocolate.
- Tea and coffee.
- Alcohol.

Sometimes, soya, spicy foods and other grains also have to be excluded in addition to foods known to cause a problem for each individual. Wheat and dairy products are the most common culprits.

## Food intolerance and exclusion diets

Food allergies are amongst the most common conditions that nutritional therapists are consulted for, and are often the cause of IBS symptoms. Many allergens are eaten frequently and are often favourite foods; this can result in chronic, sometimes debilitating effects upon health, and due to the frequent assault on our immune system, a food allergy can significantly reduce energy levels and affect immune function.

While an allergy would stimulate antibody production in the blood (this is what skin and blood tests are looking for in food allergy tests), a sensitivity or intolerance does not create the same kind of reaction. However, there is no other difference in the symptoms experienced whether you have a sensitivity, intolerance or chronic allergy to a food or drink. Hence, the term 'food allergy' is commonly used to refer to all three conditions, and the term 'allergen' used to refer to the offending food or drink.

These symptoms often accompany food allergies – if you can tick two or more, you many have an intolerance to something you regularly eat or drink:

- Fatigue (sometimes immediately after eating a specific food) or chronic fatigue, which may even be momentarily 'improved' by the allergen.
- Excess gas, flatulence, heartburn or stomach/bowel cramps.
- Diarrhoea, constipation and poor bowel movements.
- Food cravings.
- Blood sugar fluctuations.
- Atopic conditions (asthma, eczema, hayfever).

- Inflammatory conditions such as rheumatoid arthritis, IBS or ulcerative colitis.

- Moodiness, inability to concentrate, hyperactivity or depression.

While this list is not exhaustive, it includes many of the most common symptoms associated with a food allergy.

Many food allergies do not produce acute reactions, and it is very common to be unaware of symptoms or fail to link symptoms to eating certain foods. A good way to identify problem foods is to keep a food diary, simultaneously noting daily symptoms. You may be able to make a link between your symptom(s) and eating a particular food; if you can't see a connection, go to see a nutritionist or dietitian with your food diary.

It is common to be allergic or sensitive to more than one food at a time, and for this to be a long-term problem that evades diagnosis. A food allergy may be present from birth or it may suddenly occur during adult life. Food intolerance often develops over time, with initial reactions to a food ignored, and increased frequency of a specific allergen creating an 'adaptive' phase during which you may initially feel better for consuming it, and therefore unwittingly eat it more frequently. Finally, consuming the food or drink in question will no longer provide the 'quick fix' and temporary feeling of wellbeing, and you are left with the chronic fatigue and other symptoms that a food allergy or sensitivity can cause.

'To counteract symptoms of food intolerance, some people follow a rotation diet, where foods of the same "food family" are not consumed any more regularly than once every five days.'

## Will I have to avoid a food forever?

Sometimes, yes. However, often after an initial exclusion diet, during which time the gut wall can mend and become fully functional, you may find that you can take small amounts of the offending food, but less frequently than before. If you then begin to eat that food too often, the intolerance may return.

## How does an exclusion diet work?

Suspect foods and common allergens such as wheat and dairy foods are taken out of the diet and then re-introduced back into the diet one at a time. If symptoms improve while on the exclusion diet, then you have successfully removed the food causing the problems from your diet – now you need to find out which food it is! If your symptoms don't improve, then it's likely you are still eating something that is causing you problems and you may need to omit further foods from your diet.

**Important note**

It is essential that you consult a qualified nutritionist or dietitian to help you create an exclusion diet so that you are not missing any nutrients from your diet. If one food or food group is taken out of the diet, you must ensure that the nutrients normally found in these foods are replaced by alternative foods.

## How long do I have to exclude the food for?

Complete exclusion from suspect foods would normally be three weeks, although some people experience an immediate change and the cause of food intolerance is identified quite quickly. Foods which have initially been excluded but are not as likely to be causing a problem can be re-introduced sooner.

## Typical exclusion plan

Week 1 – remove wheat products, dairy products, eggs, soya products, citrus fruits, coffee, tea, alcohol and chocolate.

Week 3 – re-introduce one type of citrus fruit – if no problems occur, try another type of citrus fruit two days later.

Week 4 – re-introduce eggs. If no symptoms recur, eggs can remain in the diet. If symptoms return, then eggs are identified as an allergen and must remain excluded.

Week 5 – re-introduce another excluded food and test for symptoms. If no symptoms return, the food/drink can remain in the diet. If symptoms return, the item remains excluded.

This continues until you have a list of foods that are known to create problems and are excluded from the diet. The rest of the diet should contain a wide range of foods and not be lacking in any nutrients that the excluded food(s) contain. Sometimes the 'problem' food(s) can be re-introduced into the diet at a later stage with no problems.

'If you eat two previously excluded foods together and get a reaction, you won't know which food has caused it. You will have to re-exclude both foods and try them one at a time.'

# Dysbiosis in the bowel

Our Westernised diet, which is rich in meat, dairy produce, sugars and refined carbohydrates and generally low in fruit and vegetables, does not create a healthy bowel environment. If this describes your usual diet or you experience any of the following symptoms, which are indications of bad bowel bacteria and dysbiosis (disturbed/unhealthy bowel flora), the chances are that your bowel flora is out of balance. You can take a probiotic supplement, but this will be of little use if you continue to consume a diet that is high in protein, sugar and refined carbohydrates, and low in fibre, as you are not providing the environment for the 'good' bacteria (probiotics) to thrive in. The fibre from foods such as fruit and vegetables, beans and wholegrains provide sustenance for the 'good' bacteria to thrive on. The fibres from these foods are known as prebiotics.

Symptoms of dysbiosis include:

- Flatulence.
- Diarrhoea.
- Constipation.
- Foul smelling stools.
- Bowel cramps.
- Irregular bowel movements.
- Thrush.
- Yeast infections such as Athlete's foot or thrush.
- Severe fatigue.
- Food allergies.
- Headaches.

In a healthy gut, the 'good' bacteria normally keep unhealthy organisms in check. This helps to avoid bowel conditions which can ultimately lead to IBS and yeast infections such as candidiasis.

Several lifestyle and dietary habits can reduce the levels of healthy bacteria in our bowel, affecting the delicate balance of flora. The most common culprits are:

- Antibiotics.

- Long-term use of the contraceptive pill.

- Steroids (e.g. cortisone, contraceptive pill, hormone replacement therapy – HRT).

- Smoking.

- Stress.

- Eating large amounts of meat and dairy produce, or consuming a diet high in protein.

- Including large amounts of sugars and refined carbohydrates such as bread, biscuits or cakes.

- Regular alcohol consumption.

- Lack of dietary fibre found in fruits, vegetables and pulses.

If you can hold your hands up to more than one of these, the chances are that your bowel flora is not as healthy as it could be!

Bad bacteria thrive in the type of colonic environment created by high intakes of sugars, processed carbohydrates and eating too much protein food; an environment that is hostile to friendly bacteria. Once the unhealthy bacteria have grown in numbers, a battle between the 'good' and 'bad' bacteria determines which strains of bacteria inhabit the gut. The bacterial strains in the highest numbers create the colonic environment to suit their own growth and counteract further growth of any competing bacteria.

## Candidiasis

Candida albicans (Candida in short) is a yeast organism that naturally lives in the gut. However, poor bowel conditions create exactly the right environment for our 'good' bacteria to die off, and for organisms like Candida to grow. This overgrowth, called candidiasis, can lead to conditions such as thrush, Athlete's foot and yeast infections in the nails, mouth or stomach. Lifestyle habits that can lead to a poor bowel environment that will encourage Candida overgrowth include:

'Antibiotics kill our "good" bacteria as well as the "bad" bacteria, creating the ideal opportunity for Candida to thrive once our "good" bacteria are reduced. Many women commonly experience thrush after taking antibiotics, so much so that some GPs will advise taking a probiotic when prescribing antibiotics.'

- Lots of sugar and refined carbohydrates such as white bread – Candida feeds on sugar, so eating any type of food that increases sugar levels will feed a Candida overgrowth.

- Long-term use of the contraceptive pill or HRT – these medications have been linked with higher incidences of thrush.

- Courses of antibiotics which kill off the good bacteria as well as the bad.

- Long-term use of corticosteroid medication for rheumatoid arthritis, asthma or eczema – these drugs can depress immune function, making it easier for the Candida organism to grow.

- Regular use of non-steroidal anti-inflammatory medication – these tablets can irritate the gut lining, increasing the likelihood of a 'leaky gut' as the gut membrane becomes more porous.

- Alcohol consumption – this increases thrush as it acts in a similar way to sugar in the body.

- High intake of meat and dairy produce – this creates poor conditions for the 'good' bacteria in our bowel, but an ideal environment for other organisms such as Candida.

- Chronic stress.

Stress has an acute effect upon the gut – it can cause decreased acid production in the stomach, leading to a more alkaline environment in which Candida thrives. Stress also suppresses immune function, making it less likely that our body will fight a Candida overgrowth.

Anything that limits the growth of healthy bacteria in the bowel will produce favorable conditions for 'bad' bacteria and fungal organisms such as Candida albicans to thrive. This imbalance in our internal flora is known as dysbiosis.

There are many symptoms that might indicate Candida overgrowth – if several of these symptoms sound familiar, you may well be experiencing gut dysbiosis and/or candidiasis.

Common symptoms of candidiasis:

- Recurring cystitis.

- Oral or vaginal thrush.

- Food allergies or intolerances.

- Food cravings, especially for sugar, bread, chocolate or alcohol.

- Low blood sugar or an inability to control blood sugar levels.

- Abdominal bloating, flatulence, heartburn and indigestion.

- Poor bowel motility, diarrhoea or constipation, itchy rectum.

- Fuzzy head, inability to focus, poor concentration.

- Mood swings and depression.

- Fungal nail infections or Athletes foot.

## An anti-Candida diet

- Cut out sugars, alcohol and refined carbohydrates.

- Limit meat and dairy foods as these contribute to more unfavourable bowel conditions.

- Increase your intake of vegetables and brown rice to provide healthy fibre, which creates the ideal environment for 'good' bacteria to survive in the bowel. Examples include: inulin-rich asparagus, Jerusalem artichoke or chicory.

- Eat garlic and onion daily as these foods have anti-fungal properties and will promote the growth of 'good' bacteria in the bowel.

- Limit fruit, dried fruit and fruit juice intake – although these foods are healthy, they are still a concentrated source of sugar.

- Omit fermented products such as vinegar from your diet for the time being, and try to avoid foods which may harbor yeast organisms such as shelled nuts. If you do eat nuts, choose unshelled. Mushrooms are best omitted as they are a fungi and may encourage fungal growth.

- Try to avoid the medications listed earlier as much as possible.

- Invest in a good probiotic supplement containing Lactobacillus and Bifidobacterium species.

## Fibre

Fibre is an essential part of a healthy diet, particularly for the colon, but many IBS sufferers struggle to eat high-fibre foods. However, the type of fibre makes a big difference, as some foods are rich in 'scratchy' insoluble fibre, and other foods contain more soluble fibre which is much softer and kinder to the internal walls of the gastro-intestinal tract. Take a look at where different types of fibre are found:

| Soluble | Insoluble |
|---------|-----------|
| Fruits | Bran and cereals containing bran |
| Vegetables | Wholegrains (whole wheat, brown rice) |
| Oats and barley | Beans and pulses |

Although we need both types of fibre for health, while the intestinal wall is irritated you may need to consume foods rich in soluble fibre, which will still help to reduce constipation and improve the bowel flora and environment. There may be occasional foods which seem to agitate your condition, but cut out as few fruits and vegetables as possible, as these are the foods containing anti-inflammatory nutrients which will ultimately improve your health.

## Herbal teas

Peppermint, ginger or chamomile tea provides an alternative to normal coffee or tea and all have soothing properties which can help to alleviate heartburn, indigestion and IBS symptoms.

## Supplements

### Psyllium husk

Psyllium husk is a natural fibre that you add to water or juice. It absorbs water, creating a large, soft bolus which helps to normalise bowel function, especially helpful for constipation. Many preparations contain pre- and probiotics.

### Aloe vera

The juice of the aloe vera plant has anti-inflammatory properties that soothe the stomach and intestinal wall as it travels down the digestive tract, easing conditions such as heartburn and IBS. It also helps to correct dysbiosis.

### Digestive enzymes

Taking digestive enzymes can help you to fully digest food, although you need to discover why you are not producing your own digestive enzymes, and/or why they are not effective. You can take digestive enzymes for specific types of food to break down starches, proteins or fats, or take a supplement containing digestive enzymes for all three food groups.

### Probiotics

A good probiotic can help to re-establish the correct bowel flora in the bowel, but this has to be accompanied with a good diet so that the right environment for the 'good' bacteria is created for them to survive and grow in. Probiotic supplements are likely to be much more effective than probiotic functional foods.

### Peppermint oil or capsules

Peppermint reduces excess or spasmodic gut contractions, so peppermint in any form can help all gastro-intestinal conditions. Peppermint oil or tea may ease upper abdominal symptoms, but for IBS or constipation use coated peppermint capsules so that the peppermint is not released until it reaches the bowel.

'In independent tests carried out by the Food Standards Agency, some bacterial strains listed on probiotic food products such as yoghurt drinks were not even present, indicating absence at outset or that the bacteria had completely died off during production or storage.'

# Summing Up

Although each section of the digestive tract performs a different function and has its own ideal environment, the good news is that many dietary adaptations will help in several of the gastro-intestinal conditions discussed.

For improved digestion and bowel health:

- Eat plenty of fruit, vegetables and soluble fibre such as oats.
- If tolerated, eat lots of complex carbohydrates such as brown rice, beans and pulses.
- Limit sugar and refined carbohydrates.
- Swap coffee and tea for antioxidant-rich green tea.
- Limit alcohol intake.
- Limit protein intake from foods such as meat and dairy foods.
- For a healthy bowel, fill up on inulin-rich vegetables such as asparagus, onion, garlic and chicory.
- Include linseeds for their anti-inflammatory and bowel motility benefits.
- Drink approximately two litres of water each day for healthy bowel motility.

| Stick to... | Stay away from... |
| --- | --- |
| Fruits, oats and vegetables rich in soluble fibre. Linseeds. Inulin-rich asparagus, onion, garlic and chicory. Green, peppermint, ginger or camomile tea. Lots of water. | Refined carbohydrates and sugar. Alcohol. Large amounts of fatty, protein or spicy foods. Coffee and tea. Foods you suspect you may be intolerant of and/or common allergens. |

Need2Know

# Chapter Six

# A Diet for Great Skin

Our skin is made up of the compounds and nutrients from the food that we eat, so a healthy balanced diet is essential for good skin. Common skin complaints such as dry, rough, itchy or flaky skin can be symptoms of dehydration or fatty acid deficiency, and may respond quickly to simple dietary changes.

Eczema, dermatitis and psoriasis are common skin complaints that often respond well to nutritional medicine. With the most effective orthodox remedies such as topical steroids often causing side effects such as thinning skin, many people are searching for more natural remedies to improve skin health.

## Dermatitis

Dermatitis is a term meaning inflammation of the skin and is the same as eczema, although there are several different types.

### Allergic contact dermatitis

Allergic contact dermatitis occurs when you come into contact with a substance which your body becomes sensitised to. When you touch that substance again, your skin produces an immune reaction, creating antibodies that release chemicals such as histamine. The secretion of histamine causes symptoms like an itchy, red rash.

Common allergens which can trigger allergic contact dermatitis:

- Foods.
- Cosmetics.
- Rubber.

- Some materials.
- Some metals.
- Some plants.
- Some topical creams.

## Irritant contact dermatitis

Irritant contact dermatitis occurs when you come into contact with an irritant in detergents, soaps, perfumes, substances in toiletries or cosmetics, chemicals or some plants. As well as the usual redness, itching and inflammation, irritant contact dermatitis can cause burning, stinging and soreness. Symptoms appear immediately or within 48 hours of contact with the irritant.

In either type of dermatitis, the best way to reduce flare-ups is to identify the allergens or irritants which trigger your symptoms and then avoid these substances.

## Atopic dermatitis (eczema)

This type of dermatitis has eczematous lesions: fluid-filled structures which cause characteristic weeping. If you have eczema, you are more likely to have asthma or hayfever too, and this tendency to atopic diseases is genetically inherited. People with eczema tend to have elevated levels of certain antibodies and have difficulty in fighting off certain viral, bacterial and fungal infections, but it is often triggered by specific allergens such as soap, detergents or foods. Atopic dermatitis in particular seems to be triggered by some foods.

## Adapting your diet to counteract eczema

A number of foods have been linked with eczema:

- Dairy foods.
- Wheat and other cereals.

Need2Know

- Eggs.

- Soya products.

- Caffeine.

- Chocolate.

- Some nuts.

You might have noticed that some foods on this list keep recurring in several chapters – these are the most common allergens. In addition, some research has shown that adjusting your intake of fatty acids may also improve eczema.

## Excluding suspect foods

Many skin conditions, particularly eczema, respond well when allergens such as hens' eggs or dairy foods are excluded from the diet. Although many scientific trials include small numbers of people and a definitive conclusion cannot be reached about the effectiveness of exclusion diets for skin conditions, you may think it's worth a try to see if changing your diet affects your skin condition.

A number of foods can all be excluded on the same diet – exclude them all in one go at the start and then bring them back into your diet one at a time to test them. It will help to keep a note of which foods you try and the reactions that you experience – this will enable you to create a list of foods that you know you can eat, and a list of foods to avoid as they worsen your eczema. Try to stay on the exclusion diet for inflammatory skin conditions (see chapter 7) for up to three weeks and then re-introduce one food at a time, in order of the foods you think are least likely to cause a problem. This way, you'll be able to widen the variety of foods in your diet more quickly.

Overleaf is an example of initially excluded foods that could be re-introduced back into the diet one at a time. Foods or drinks that cause no problems or skin flare-ups are left in the diet once re-introduced, but anything that worsens or causes symptoms is taken back out of the diet.

'Eczema sufferers may benefit from excluding cow's milk products from the diet. Yet they may be able to consume products made with sheep or goat's milk without any detrimental effects to their skin condition.'

| Foods to try | Date tried | Comments |
| --- | --- | --- |
| Coffee with no milk | | |
| Bread | | |
| Eggs | | |
| Sheep or goat yoghurt | | |
| Sheep or goat's milk | | |
| Cow's milk and yoghurt | | |

Need2Know

# Adjusting your fatty acid intake

As well as following an exclusion diet, an anti-inflammatory diet is also recommended as eczema is an inflammatory skin condition. Adjusting the ratio of fatty acids by increasing the amount of omega 3 fats while reducing the amount of omega 6 fats is particularly recommended. Vegetarian diets have also shown positive results on inflammatory skin disorders.

To eat more fats with anti-inflammatory properties, you should:

- Eat more oily fish such as tuna, salmon, pilchards, mackerel and sardines.

- Eat more tinned fish and white fish such as cod, haddock and plaice – they also contain omega 3 fats, although not as much as the oily fish.

- Eat more linseeds and walnuts; they are rich sources of alpha-linolenic acid, which the body can convert into the long-chain fatty acids found in fish.

- Stop using safflower or sunflower vegetable oils as these contain more omega 6 fats which limit the conversion of non-fish omega 3 into long-chain fatty acids.

- Use linseed or rapeseed oil for salad dressings as it has a good omega 3 to omega 6 ratio.

If you don't eat much fish, it can be difficult to consume enough omega 3, especially as the conversion rate from non-fish sources can be low. Therefore, a fatty acid supplement may be helpful – look for eicosapentaenoic acid (EPA) and docosahexaenoic acid (DHA), and take 1,000mg (1g) daily.

# Oolong tea

Some research indicates that the plant nutrients found in tea may have beneficial effects upon skin conditions. One research study (Uehara *et al.*, 2001) found that 63% of patients who drank one litre of oolong tea each day (three equal servings after each meal) showed marked to moderate improvement within one month of treatment. Green (and black) tea also contains therapeutic nutrients with anti-inflammatory properties.

### Zinc

Zinc deficiency is common in acne and eczema sufferers, and plays a major role in skin health and immune function. Zinc is found in meats (particularly the dark cuts of meat), oysters, offal, wholegrains, pumpkin seeds, asparagus and watercress. If you think it's going to be difficult to increase your zinc intake (for example, if you are vegetarian), take a multi-mineral containing at least 15mg of zinc.

# Psoriasis

The prevalence of psoriasis in Western populations is estimated to be around 2-3%, and despite several different types of treatment including orthodox medicines, phototherapy (treatment with sunlight/UV light) and ichthyotherapy (where 'doctor fish' eat the psoriatic plaques), there appears be no actual cure.

The cause of psoriasis is still unknown, although there appears to be a genetic tendency and an irregularity in immune regulation. Psoriasis is characterised by red, scaly patches on the skin, caused by excessive skin production and inflammation. It normally takes approximately one month for skin cells to form the outer layer of skin, but this process is accelerated in psoriasis, creating too much skin which pushes together forming crusts and plaques.

Certain foods may trigger flare-ups of psoriasis, and factors that also aggravate psoriasis include:

- Stress.
- Alcohol.
- Smoking.
- Withdrawal of systemic corticosteroids (medication to reduce inflammation).

As well as finding ways to reduce or manage stress more effectively, stopping smoking and reducing alcohol intake will also help your psoriasis. In addition to these lifestyle adjustments, there are a number of dietary changes that you can try.

There are several elements to consider in a therapeutic diet for psoriasis. Ideally, you need to:

- Support your immune system with antioxidants.

- Follow an anti-inflammatory diet.

- Consider following an exclusion diet to encourage optimal intestinal and bowel function – this will also support liver function and natural detoxification, easing the workload on the immune system.

- Avoid foods that may trigger flare-ups of psoriasis (see page 119 for examples).

- Ensure a rich source of certain vitamins and minerals in the diet.

Although this may seem like lots of different dietary adjustments, most of these changes are helpful in more than one way. For example, antioxidants such as vitamin E and selenium are also anti-inflammatory and will support liver function, and the foods rich in antioxidants are also those that support healthy intestinal and bowel function.

## Support immune function with antioxidants

If you have psoriasis, there are several reasons to eat a diet rich in antioxidants such as vitamins C and E, selenium, zinc and beta carotene. These nutrients are helpful in most skin conditions, so tips on how to eat more zinc, beta carotene and vitamin E can be found in the sections on eczema and acne. You can increase your antioxidant intake in three ways:

- Follow the tips given in this chapter or follow the eating plan given in chapter 7, filling up on foods rich in beta carotene, vitamins C and E, and minerals such as zinc and selenium.

- Eat a healthy diet and support it with a multi-vitamin, multi-mineral to boost nutrient intake further.

- Consult a qualified nutritional therapist or dietitian who will be able to provide a specific diet and prescribe a therapeutic nutrient supplementation plan.

## Vitamin C

Vitamin C has anti-inflammatory properties, so any inflammatory skin condition may benefit from therapeutic doses of this vitamin. Both vitamin C and vitamin E also support and help to normalise immune function. Foods rich in vitamin C include citrus fruits, berries, green leafy vegetables, peppers, kiwi fruit and potatoes.

To increase your dietary intake of vitamin C, you should:

- Add berries and kiwi to breakfast cereals.
- Add rocket to pasta and rice dishes.
- Add watercress or spinach to salads and sandwiches.

'It's better to place potatoes directly into boiling water as they lose much of their vitamin C content at lower temperatures.'

## Selenium

As well as being an important anti-inflammatory and antioxidant, selenium is required for the detoxification process, so it helps to reduce toxin levels in the skin. It works with vitamin E, so it's a good idea to take these two antioxidants together. Foods rich in selenium include Brazil nuts, sunflower seeds, wholegrain cereals, seafood and offal.

To increase your dietary intake of selenium, you should:

- Snack on nuts, particularly Brazil nuts.
- Enjoy a prawn sandwich or crab salad for lunch.
- Increase seafood intake with paella or scallops.

## Eat an anti-inflammatory diet

Due to the inflammatory nature of skin conditions, it makes sense to fill up on foods that contain nutrients with anti-inflammatory properties, as outlined in the anti-inflammatory diet for rheumatoid arthritis in chapter 2. These include:

- Fish, nuts and seeds rich in omega 3 fatty acids.
- Onions.

■ Green leafy vegetables.

To swap pro-inflammatory foods for anti-inflammatory foods, you should:

■ Swap meat, eggs or cheese for fresh or tinned fish in sandwiches.

■ Swap cheese on toast to sardines on toast.

■ Swap breakfast omelette or eggs to kedgeree.

■ Swap roast meats at dinner for salmon or tuna steak.

■ Use tuna or soya mince in place of mince in pasta dishes.

■ Add linseeds and walnuts to cereals, yoghurts, salads and stir-fries.

■ Try bars with added seeds such as the 9Bar with linseeds.

■ Snack on walnuts.

■ Add rocket, watercress or spinach to sandwiches and salads.

■ Add cabbage or spinach to rice and pasta dishes.

■ Eat onions every day – add to sandwiches, salads and omelettes. Base each cooked meal on onions.

## Try an exclusion diet

There are several reasons to find an exclusion diet that suits you if you suffer with psoriasis.

■ Research has made several links between psoriasis and dysfunction in the digestive tract and bowel.

■ Studies also show potential links between psoriasis occuring with arthritis and gout, both of which flare up with specific foods.

■ There are significant links between gluten intolerance and psoriasis.

## The bowel-liver connection

Several studies have illustrated links between psoriasis, poor digestive function and poor bowel health, supporting potential links with gluten intolerance and the idea that exclusion diets may improve the condition. Research also indicates higher occurrence of non-alcoholic fatty liver disease in psoriasis patients, indicating that dietary adjustments benefitting bowel and liver function may be helpful.

## Links with arthritis or gout

The UK Psoriasis Association states that up to 40% of people with severe psoriasis have psoriatic arthritis. There may also be links between the development of rheumatoid arthritis or gout and psoriasis, indicating that dietary adaptations that suit these conditions may also benefit psoriasis.

Gout is caused by a build up of uric acid in the blood, formed from the break down of purines, chemical compounds found in some foods. Uric acid is usually removed from the body in the urine, but excess uric acid forms crystals which accumulate in the joints and cause the symptoms of gout. As there may be links between psoriasis and gout, you may benefit from reducing these purine-rich foods in your diet:

- Game, meat and offal.
- Herrings, sardines, shellfish and fish roe.
- Sugars and refined carbohydrates.
- Fruit.
- Yeast.
- Alcohol.

## Links with gluten

Some studies have shown improvement in psoriasis with a gluten-free diet. Part of the gluten found in cereals such as wheat, rye or oats is called gliadin – this is what people with coeliac disease react to, with the result of breaking out in pustular skin eruptions similar to psoriasis. Psoriasis sufferers often have slightly more anti-gliadin antibodies than the general population, so following a gluten-free diet may be worth a try.

However, to avoid gluten completely means taking most grains out of the diet – no bread, oats, pasta, couscous, biscuits or cakes unless made with gluten-free flour. But if you want to try a few days to see how your psoriasis reacts, you could try a gluten-free eating plan like the one shown below.

## Monday

| | |
|---|---|
| Breakfast | Soya yoghurt with added linseeds and fruit. |
| Mid-morning | A piece of fruit or raw vegetables. |
| Lunch | Tomato soup and a small salad (see chapter 8). |
| Dinner | Baked salmon steak with asparagus, carrots and baked sweet potato. |

## Tuesday

| | |
|---|---|
| Breakfast | Fruit salad – apple, pear, banana, grapes, mango. |
| Mid-morning | Asparagus, carrot and pepper slices with homemade hummus (see chapter 8). |
| Lunch | Mixed bean and brown rice salad (see chapter 8). |
| Dinner | Seared tuna steak with roasted root vegetables (see chapter 8). |

## Wednesday

| | |
|---|---|
| Breakfast | Gluten-free cereal with added linseeds and fruit. |
| Mid-morning | Cherry tomatoes, baby corn and carrot with homemade hummus (see chapter 8). |
| Lunch | Salmon with spinach, onion, garlic, carrots, tomatoes and beetroot. |

| Dinner | Chilli bean casserole with jacket or roasted potatoes (see chapter 8). |

## Thursday

| Breakfast | Poached eggs on a bed of spinach. |
| Mid-morning | Lentil soup. |
| Lunch | Baked potato with tuna and a mixed salad. |
| Dinner | Vegetable stir-fries with red cabbage, red onion, garlic and mushrooms, plus any other vegetables you like. |

## Friday

| Breakfast | Gluten-free bread toasted, spread with ripe avocado. |
| Mid-morning | Nut bar. |
| Lunch | Lentil soup. |
| Dinner | Stuffed vegetables (see chapter 8). |

You can try the gluten-free eating plan above for up to a week to see how it may affect your psoriasis, but after that you should consult a dietitian or nutritionist for a long-term eating plan that contains enough carbohydrate foods, as it is largely this food group that you exclude on a gluten-free diet. However, if you wish to simply reduce your gluten intake and try a wheat-free diet, you could follow the seven day eating plan in chapter 7.

## Avoid trigger foods

Most of the common trigger foods are not included in a healthy exclusion diet; however, your trigger foods may be different to someone else's, so exclude any foods that seem to cause a flare up in symptoms, but include any healthy trigger foods that don't cause you a problem. There's little point including cola drinks or monosodium glutamate (also known as MSG – a flavour enhancer found commonly in processed foods) as they won't benefit your overall health, but tomatoes and berries contain important nutrients known to benefit health, so you should eat them if you can.

Trigger foods for psoriasis are thought to include these foods:

- Red meat.
- Refined carbohydrates and bakery goods – white bread, cakes, biscuits, etc.
- Cola.
- Red wine (and alcohol generally).
- Monosodium glutamate.
- Chilli and other hot spices.
- Berries.
- Tomatoes.

## Water

Water is vital for efficient metabolism and to help rid the body of toxins and waste products – without adequate hydration, our skin can look and feel dry. An easy way to tell if you are dehydrated is by checking the colour of your urine – if it is a pale straw colour, you are hydrated; if it is too dark, you need to drink more water. Adequate hydration is an essential part of a therapeutic diet for psoriasis.

To increase your water intake you should:

- Drink a filled one-and-a-half or two litre bottle throughout the day – a great way to measure how much you're drinking.
- Drink herbal teas or hot water with a slice of lemon or lime as a refreshing alternative to coffee or tea.
- Take a small bottle of water with you when you go out in the car or on a walk so you always have something to drink.

'You can calculate your water requirements based upon your body weight – you need 35ml of water for every kg of bodyweight, so if you weigh 60kg, you need 35ml x 60kg = 2,100ml (2.1 litres) of water daily.'

- Re-hydrate during and after exercise as you have to replace the water that you have lost as sweat.

- Fill up on foods with high water content such as melons, cucumber, tomatoes and pears.

## Vitamin D

We make vitamin D in the skin when we expose our skin to the sunlight. As psoriasis markedly improves in the sun, large doses of vitamin D has been used in dermatology for the treatment of psoriasis.

You can increase the vitamin D in your diet by eating more oily fish, eggs, liver, margarines and cereals fortified with vitamin D.

However, as eggs, liver, margarines and some cereals are limited in a therapeutic diet for psoriasis, top up vitamin D levels with a little sunshine and a good multi-vitamin supplement.

## Supplements

Supplements that may help psoriasis include:

- Lecithin and milk thistle which both support liver function.

- A good probiotic will enhance your bowel flora – try this and also follow other recommendations for a healthy bowel in chapter 5.

# Acne

Acne is characterised by inflammatory and non-inflammatory spots and pimples caused by hair follicles blocked with plugs of sebum and dead skin cells. Production of sebum from the sebaceous glands in the skin is affected by secretion of androgen (sex) hormones, and there is a link between higher testosterone levels and acne (in females and males).

There can be a number of causes:

- Family history.

- Increased/altered hormonal activity. For example, during puberty or menopause, or as a result of taking anabolic steroids.

- As a result of hormonal changes due to other medical conditions such as polycystic ovarian syndrome.

- Over secretion of sebum, usually linked to hormone (testosterone) levels.

Stress can make acne worse, and there are a number of links between diet and acne. The following dietary habits could cause or contribute to your acne:

- Too many high-GI carbohydrates such as cakes, biscuits and white flour products.

- Milk and other dairy products.

- Low intakes of vitamins A and E.

## Adapting your diet to counteract acne

Although there has been a long held assumption that a diet high in 'junk food' causes acne, more research in this area has identified more specific food groups that appear to contribute to this skin condition. In fact, research states that the effects of chocolate on acne are 'inconclusive' as it neither improved nor worsened the condition, unlike other foods with high sugar levels.

## High-GI carbohydrates

Carbohydrates which cause high sugar levels and stimulate insulin secretion have been linked with acne. Insulin triggers the release of insulin-like growth factor (IGF), which in turn affects the sebaceous glands, skin secretion and metabolism. Insulin resistance, which causes elevated blood sugar and high insulin levels, is found in polycystic ovarian syndrome, where acne is also a common complaint. To avoid high blood sugar levels, eat foods that release sugars slowly into the bloodstream.

- Swap white bread for rye, wholemeal or GI bread.

- Exclude biscuits, muffins, pastries and cakes from your diet. Instead, eat oat or nut-based snacks.

- Eat fruit instead of sweets.
- Use a GI counter book such as *Collins Gem GI* (Harper Collins).

## Dairy

There appears to be a link between acne and the consumption of milk and other dairy products, although researchers suggest this may be due to the effects of hormones in the dairy produce rather than the food itself. If this is the case, it may be worth trying these alternatives:

- Swap to organic milk.
- Consume milk products from sheep or goats.
- Use soya, oat or rice milk.

'Large, well-controlled research studies have demonstrated an association between cow's milk intake and acne prevalence and severity.'

## Vitamins

Studies have shown that newly diagnosed acne patients sometimes have lower levels of vitamin A and vitamin E. Adequate amounts of vitamin A naturally inhibit sebum secretion from the sebaceous glands, and many acne medications are based upon vitamin A (retinol) therapy. However, these have a number of side effects, and when treatment finishes the acne often reappears.

As well as having an anti-inflammatory role in acne control, vitamin A reduces the creation of acne lesions by reducing clogged pores and modifying how dead skin cells are removed.

Food sources of vitamin A include milk, cheese, eggs and beef or chicken liver. However, vitamin A is a fat soluble vitamin which is stored in the liver, so to avoid excess amounts being stored it is safer to eat more foods rich in beta carotene.

# Beta carotene

Beta carotene can be converted into vitamin A as and when your body needs it. Any excess beta carotene is largely removed in urine, which is better for you because any excess will not be stored in the liver. Beta carotene has also been proven to offer skin protection to sun exposure. Foods rich in beta carotene include:

- Sweet potato.
- Carrots.
- Squash.
- Pumpkin.
- Mango.
- Papaya.
- Apricots.
- Green leafy vegetables.
- Beetroot.

For healthy skin and to reduce acne, pack your diet out with beta carotene-rich foods, particularly during the summer to enhance skin protection. An example of a diet rich in beta carotene is shown below.

## Breakfasts

Blend cantaloupe melon and peaches with soya yoghurt or banana and a little linseed or rapeseed oil for a beta carotene smoothie.

## Lunches

Corn tortilla wrap with spinach, avocado, peppers, grated carrots, tomatoes, beetroot and pumpkin seeds.

## Dinners

Salmon with asparagus, roasted carrots and sweet potato.

## Snacks

Apricots, mangos, peaches or nectarines.

Heavy cooking can destroy much of the beta carotene in vegetables, but light cooking, mashing or puréeing may enhance its availability and absorption as the plant cell walls are broken and open up to release the beta carotene within. It is best absorbed with some fat in the meal, so combine orange fruits with seeds or nuts, and orange vegetables with a little olive oil.

## Vitamin E

Vitamin E is another fat soluble vitamin often linked with skin health. Vitamin E supplementation has antioxidant, anti-inflammatory and immune-supportive properties, and eczema and dry, itchy skin have also been linked with a deficiency of this vitamin.

Vitamin E can improve the condition of your skin because:

- It supports immune function, which is over-stimulated in eczema, dermatitis and acne.

- It reduces free radical damage, which is a significant cause of ageing (and explains why it's found in so many face and body creams).

- By reducing free radical damage it can reduce the occurrence of liver spots commonly associated with ageing.

Foods rich in vitamin E include vegetable oils, nuts (especially almonds, Brazil nuts and hazelnuts), pine nuts, sunflower seeds, avocado and wheat germ.

To increase your dietary intake of vitamin E, you should try:

- Snacking on nuts and seeds.

- Drizzling high quality, cold vegetable oils onto salads.

- Adding pine nuts to salads and stir-fries.

- Adding wheat germ to cereals or yoghurts.

- Adding avocado to salad sandwiches, salads and wraps.

Vitamin E works in conjunction with vitamin C, the effects of each vitamin increased by the other, so a healthy diet should be rich in both of these antioxidants.

## Phytoestrogens

Because there is a link between acne and elevated testosterone levels (a male hormone), and phytoestrogens can mimic or modulate the activity of the female hormone oestrogen and reduce testosterone levels, including foods rich in phytoestrogens in your diet may be beneficial.

Foods rich in phytoestrogens include:

- Soya products such as soya beans, soya milk, soya yoghurt and tofu.

- Chickpeas, lentils and mung beans.

- Fruits such as apples, plums and cherries.

- Peppers, yams, tomatoes, olives, carrots, fennel, potatoes and aubergine.

To add phytoestrogen-rich foods to your diet, you could:

- Replace dairy milk and yoghurt with soya milk and yoghurt.

- Snack on plums, cherries and apples.

- Use soya mince instead of beef to make lasagne or spaghetti bolognese.

- Snack on hummus (made with chickpeas).

- Use soya beans as a vegetable staple.

# Summing Up

There are a number of nutrients required for healthy skin. Creating a healthy diet based upon these elements will improve the overall condition of skin, as well as improve many skin conditions.

- Eat the right ratio of fatty acids – more omega 3, less omega 6.

- Exclude common allergens such as dairy and wheat from your diet.

- Include lots of antioxidant-rich foods to reduce inflammation and promote healthy skin formation and function.

- Eat low-GI carbohydrates and cut down on refined carbohydrates.

- Drink plenty of water – up to two litres every day.

| Stick to... | Stay away from... |
|---|---|
| Lots of water. | Dairy, wheat, eggs and common allergens. |
| Low-GI carbohydrates. | |
| Antioxidant-rich foods for vitamins A, C and E, zinc and selenium. | Refined carbohydrates. |
| Omega 3-rich foods – fish, linseeds and walnuts. | |

# Chapter Seven

# Therapeutic Eating Plans

## Hypertension and atherosclerosis

### Monday

| | |
|---|---|
| Breakfast | Porridge made with soya milk, plus added linseeds and fruit. |
| Mid-morning | Celery, asparagus and radish with homemade hummus (see chapter 8). |
| Lunch | Tomato soup and a green salad (see chapter 8). |
| Dinner | Baked salmon steak with broccoli, cauliflower and baked sweet potato. |

### Tuesday

| | |
|---|---|
| Breakfast | Soya yoghurt with flaked almonds, linseeds and cherries. |
| Mid-morning | Celery and pepper sticks. |
| Lunch | Mixed bean and brown rice salad (see chapter 8). |
| Dinner | Seared tuna steak with roast potatoes, parsnips, carrots and broccoli. |

### Wednesday

| | |
|---|---|
| Breakfast | Granola mixed with oats and fruit. |
| Mid-morning | Soya yoghurt sprinkled with linseeds and mixed berries. |
| Lunch | Sardines with chicory, onion, garlic, asparagus, celery and beetroot. |
| Dinner | Savoy cabbage stir-fry with brown rice (see chapter 8). |

## Thursday

| | |
|---|---|
| Breakfast | Porridge with soya milk, plus added almonds, linseeds and fruit. |
| Mid-morning | Oatcakes and homemade hummus, celery, peppers and carrot (see chapter 8). |
| Lunch | Peppered mackerel with a large mixed salad with chicory. |
| Dinner | Stuffed vegetables with a large green salad (see chapter 8). |

## Friday

| | |
|---|---|
| Breakfast | Fruit salad with soya yoghurt and mixed seeds. |
| Mid-morning | Fresh fruit or raw vegetables. |
| Lunch | Mixed bean and brown rice salad (see chapter 8). |
| Dinner | Superfood curry with brown rice (see chapter 8). |

## Saturday

| | |
|---|---|
| Breakfast | Granola mixed with oats or millet. |
| Snacks | Celery, peppers and carrot sticks with homemade hummus (see chapter 8). |
| Lunch | Tomato and lentil soup (see chapter 8). |
| Dinner | Steamed fish with potatoes, carrots and asparagus. |

## Sunday

| | |
|---|---|
| Breakfast | Kedgeree (see chapter 8). |
| Mid-morning | Homemade hummus with celery, radish and tomatoes (see chapter 8). |
| Lunch | Sunday roast (with plenty of vegetables and low salt gravy). |
| Dinner | Watercress or broccoli soup with oatcakes. |

*... and maybe an occasional glass of red wine if you're having a tipple!*

# Rheumatoid arthritis or osteoarthritis

## Monday

| | |
|---|---|
| Breakfast | Porridge with soya milk, linseeds and banana. |
| Mid-morning | A piece of fruit – apple, pear, apricot or peach. |
| Lunch | Watercress soup with oatcakes. |
| Dinner | Seared tuna steak with broccoli, cauliflower and roasted squash. |

## Tuesday

| | |
|---|---|
| Breakfast | Millet or oat flakes with soya yoghurt, walnuts and linseeds. |
| Mid-morning | Raw carrot and pepper sticks with homemade hummus (see chapter 8). |
| Lunch | Corn tortilla wrap with salad – rocket, cucumber, radish, celery and avocado with added walnuts and linseed oil. |
| Dinner | Baked salmon steak with carrots, broccoli and baked sweet potato. |

## Wednesday

| | |
|---|---|
| Breakfast | Banana smoothie with linseed oil and soya yoghurt. |
| Mid-morning | Oatcakes and raw vegetables with homemade hummus (see chapter 8). |
| Lunch | Mixed bean and brown rice salad (see chapter 8). |
| Dinner | Savoy cabbage stir-fry with rice noodles (see chapter 8). |

## Thursday

| | |
|---|---|
| Breakfast | Porridge with soya milk, fruit, linseeds and walnuts. |
| Mid-morning | Cherries and/or red grapes with soya yoghurt. |
| Lunch | Sardines with a large green salad, beetroot, carrot and onion. |
| Dinner | Tofu and brown rice vegetable risotto. |

## Friday

| | |
|---|---|
| Breakfast | Granola with soya milk. |
| Mid-morning | Celery, raw peppers and carrot sticks with homemade hummus (see chapter 8). |
| Lunch | Jacket potato with tinned or poached salmon and side salad. |
| Dinner | Chilli bean casserole (see chapter 8). |

## Saturday

| | |
|---|---|
| Breakfast | Oat or millet flake porridge with soya milk and added linseeds. |
| Snacks | Raw vegetables or fruit. |
| Lunch | Vegetable soup with oatcakes. |
| Dinner | Steamed lemon sole or trout with potatoes and vegetables. |

## Sunday

| | |
|---|---|
| Breakfast | Kedgeree (see chapter 8). |
| Mid-morning | Fresh fruit salad. |
| Lunch | Sunday roast (with plenty of vegetables but little or no meat). |
| Dinner | Watercress or broccoli soup with oatcakes. |

*... and add anti-inflammatory turmeric or ginger to foods every day.*

# Osteoporosis

## Monday

| | |
|---|---|
| Breakfast | Oatabix made with soya milk, soya yoghurt and fruit. |
| Mid-morning | A piece of fruit – apple, plum or cherries. |
| Lunch | Jacket potato with hummus or tinned sardines and rocket. |
| Dinner | Seared lean beef steak with broccoli, cauliflower and roasted squash. |

## Tuesday

| | |
|---|---|
| Breakfast | Muesli with soya milk, soya yoghurt, walnuts and linseeds. |
| Mid-morning | Olives or nuts. |
| Lunch | Chicken sandwich on wholemeal bread with mixed salad vegetables including spinach and rocket. |
| Dinner | Turkey stir-fry with chickpeas and vegetables, served with brown rice. |

## Wednesday

| | |
|---|---|
| Breakfast | Porridge with soya milk, mixed seeds and fruit. |
| Mid-morning | Oatcakes and raw vegetables with homemade hummus (see chapter 8). |
| Lunch | Mixed bean and brown rice salad (see chapter 8). |
| Dinner | Baked salmon steak with carrots, broccoli and baked sweet potato. |

## Thursday

| | |
|---|---|
| Breakfast | Poached egg on a bed of spinach. |
| Mid-morning | Cherries, plums or apple with soya yoghurt. |
| Lunch | Sardines with a large green salad, beetroot, carrot and onion. |
| Dinner | Tofu and brown rice vegetable risotto. |

### Friday

| | |
|---|---|
| Breakfast | Granola with soya milk. |
| Mid-morning | Olives or nuts. |
| Lunch | Watercress soup with oatcakes. |
| Dinner | Superfood curry and brown rice (see chapter 8). |

### Saturday

| | |
|---|---|
| Breakfast | Omelette with wilted spinach, mixed peppers and red onion. |
| Snacks | Raw vegetables or fruit. |
| Lunch | Homemade vegetable soup with oatcakes. |
| Dinner | Steamed lemon sole or trout with soya beans and vegetables. |

### Sunday

| | |
|---|---|
| Breakfast | Wholemeal bread toasted with peanut butter or tahini. |
| Mid-morning | Fresh fruit salad. |
| Lunch | Sunday roast (chicken, salmon steak or nut roast). |
| Dinner | Mixed green salad with pine nuts, olives and tomatoes. |

*... and this is one condition where a milky drink may help!*

# Diabetes and insulin resistance

## Monday

Breakfast — Porridge with soya milk. Add cinnamon, seeds or flaked nuts and berries.

Mid-morning — A piece of fruit – apple, kiwi or dried apricots with soya yoghurt.

Lunch — Tomato and lentil soup with pumpernickel, rye or sourdough bread (see chapter 8).

Dinner — Baked salmon steak with avocado and a large mixed salad.

## Tuesday

Breakfast — Soya or live yoghurt with cinnamon, flaked almonds and cherries.

Mid-morning — Celery or pepper sticks with homemade hummus (see chapter 8).

Lunch — Chicken, turkey or hummus salad sandwich on low-GI bread.

Dinner — Brown rice vegetable risotto with garlic and onion.

## Wednesday

Breakfast — Muesli with added mixed seeds and orange or grapefruit.

Mid-morning — A nut or seed bar.

Lunch — Leftover brown rice vegetable risotto (cook a little extra for dinner on Tuesday).

Dinner — Stuffed vegetables (see chapter 8).

## Thursday

Breakfast — Kedgeree (see chapter 8).

Mid-morning — Cherries and/or red grapes with soya yoghurt.

Lunch — Egg or salmon salad sandwich on pumpernickel, rye or sourdough bread.

Dinner — Turkey or tofu and vegetable stir-fry.

### Friday

| | |
|---|---|
| Breakfast | Granola mixed with oats, flaked almonds and berries, served with soya milk and dusted with cinnamon. |
| Mid-morning | A nut or seed bar. |
| Lunch | Jacket potato with salad, chicken, hummus or tuna. |
| Dinner | Bean and vegetable stew with brown rice. |

### Saturday

| | |
|---|---|
| Breakfast | Omelette with mushrooms, onions and peppers, served with grilled tomatoes. |
| Snacks | A handful of dried apricots and nuts. |
| Lunch | Lentil soup. |
| Dinner | Steamed fish with roasted squash, asparagus and mange tout. |

### Sunday

| | |
|---|---|
| Breakfast | Porridge with soya milk. Add cinnamon, seeds or flaked nuts and berries. |
| Mid-morning | Oatcakes and homemade hummus with raw vegetables (see chapter 8). |
| Lunch | Sunday roast. |
| Dinner | Watercress or broccoli soup with oatcakes. |

*... and drink green tea as desired!*

# Premenstrual syndrome

## Monday

Breakfast — Porridge made with soya milk with added linseeds, pumpkin seeds, dried apricots and cherries.

Mid-morning — Oatcake and homemade hummus with celery, apple, carrot and radish.

Lunch — Cauliflower and lentil soup.

Dinner — Chilli bean casserole served with brown rice (see chapter 8).

## Tuesday

Breakfast — Mixed fruit salad (berries, mango, apricots, peach, red grapes) with soya yoghurt and pumpkin seeds.

Mid-morning — Asparagus and pepper sticks with homemade hummus (see chapter 8).

Lunch — Mixed bean and brown rice salad (see chapter 8).

Dinner — Seared tuna steak and garlic-roasted root vegetables, with cauliflower.

## Wednesday

Breakfast — Granola with soya yoghurt, chopped plums and cherries.

Mid-morning — A nut or seed bar.

Lunch — Jacket potato with homemade hummus and salad.

Dinner — Savoy cabbage stir-fry (see chapter 8).

## Thursday

Breakfast — Porridge with soya milk, added mixed seeds and plums.

Mid-morning — Olives and nuts.

Lunch — Mackerel served on oatcakes with salad vegetables.

Dinner — Brown rice vegetable risotto.

## Friday

| | |
|---|---|
| Breakfast | Soya yoghurt with kiwi, cherries, almonds and pumpkin seeds. |
| Mid-morning | Tomatoes, raw peppers and carrot sticks with homemade hummus (see chapter 8). |
| Lunch | Lentil soup with oatcakes. |
| Dinner | Superfood curry with brown rice (see chapter 8). |

## Saturday

| | |
|---|---|
| Breakfast | Granola with wheat germ, soya yoghurt and chopped plums and cherries. |
| Snacks | A nut or seed bar. |
| Lunch | Corn tortilla wrap with mixed green leaves, carrots, beetroot, red onion, mozzarella cheese and avocado. |
| Dinner | Steamed fish, garlic-roasted squash, aubergine and broccoli. |

## Sunday

| | |
|---|---|
| Breakfast | Poached egg on wholemeal toast. |
| Mid-morning | Olives and tomatoes with oatcakes. |
| Lunch | Sunday roast. |
| Dinner | Avocado on toasted seed bread with green leaf and walnut salad and a linseed oil dressing. |

*... and a little bit of dark chocolate when necessary!*

# To improve mood and cognitive function

## Monday

| | |
|---|---|
| Breakfast | Porridge with soya milk, mixed seeds and raspberries. |
| Mid-morning | Oatcake and homemade hummus with celery, apple, carrot and radish (see chapter 8). |
| Lunch | Peppered mackerel with a green leafy salad, beetroot, tomatoes, red onion and grated carrot and seeded bread. |
| Dinner | Chilli bean casserole (see chapter 8). |

## Tuesday

| | |
|---|---|
| Breakfast | Fruit salad with mixed berries, mango, apricots, peach, kiwi and red grapes, with soya or live yoghurt and mixed seeds. |
| Mid-morning | Celery, carrot and pepper sticks with cherry tomatoes. |
| Lunch | Mixed bean and brown rice salad (see chapter 8). |
| Dinner | Tofu stir-fry with vegetables. |

## Wednesday

| | |
|---|---|
| Breakfast | Granola with cherries and apricots. |
| Mid-morning | A nut or seed bar. |
| Lunch | Sardines on wholemeal toast with a dark green leafy salad. |
| Dinner | Savoy cabbage stir-fry (see chapter 8). |

## Thursday

| | |
|---|---|
| Breakfast | Omega 3 fortified boiled egg with toasted wholemeal bread. |
| Mid-morning | A handful of nuts. |
| Lunch | Lentil soup and oatcakes. |
| Dinner | Salmon and sweet potato risotto with rocket or spinach (see chapter 8). |

### Friday

| | |
|---|---|
| Breakfast | Soya yoghurt, kiwi, cherries, raspberries, almonds and pumpkin seeds. |
| Mid-morning | Tomatoes, raw peppers and carrot sticks with homemade hummus (see chapter 8). |
| Lunch | Corn tortilla wrap with turkey, bean sprouts, watercress and avocado. |
| Dinner | Tuna steak with olive oil roasted squash, carrots and broccoli. |

### Saturday

| | |
|---|---|
| Breakfast | Poached omega 3 fortified egg on wholemeal toast. |
| Snacks | A handful of cherries. |
| Lunch | Lentil soup and oatcakes. |
| Dinner | Baked fish or organic meat with roast vegetables and cabbage. |

### Sunday

| | |
|---|---|
| Breakfast | Kedgeree (see chapter 8). |
| Mid-morning | Soya yoghurt with kiwi, orange segments and pumpkin seeds. |
| Lunch | Sunday roast. |
| Dinner | Avocado on toasted seed bread with watercress and walnut salad, linseed dressing. |

*... and drink red/purple coloured fruit juice – cranberry, acai berry or red grape juice.*

# Heartburn, indigestion and IBS

## Monday

| | |
|---|---|
| Breakfast | Banana smoothie with soya yoghurt, soya milk and linseeds. |
| Mid-morning | Homemade hummus and raw vegetables (see chapter 8). |
| Lunch | Homemade tomato soup with oatcakes and salad (see chapter 8). |
| Dinner | Salmon and sweet potato risotto with wilted spinach (see chapter 8). |

## Tuesday

| | |
|---|---|
| Breakfast | Granola with soya, rice or oat milk or water, linseeds and apple. |
| Mid-morning | A nut or seed bar. |
| Lunch | Corn tortilla wrap with bean sprouts, cucumber, radish, onion, watercress and avocado. |
| Dinner | Tofu stir-fry with vegetables and brown rice. |

## Wednesday

| | |
|---|---|
| Breakfast | Porridge with soya, oat or rice milk or water, with banana and linseeds. |
| Mid-morning | Fruit – cherries, peaches, apricots or apples. |
| Lunch | Jacket potato with hummus and salad. |
| Dinner | Savoy cabbage stir-fry with added garlic and tofu or chicken (see chapter 8). |

## Thursday

| | |
|---|---|
| Breakfast | Fruit salad with mixed berries, mango, apricots, peach, banana and red grapes with mixed seeds. |
| Mid-morning | A gluten- or wheat-free nut or seed bar. |

| | |
|---|---|
| Lunch | Sardines with a large green salad dressed with linseed or walnut oil, onion, asparagus and beetroot. |
| Dinner | Steamed fish with roasted squash, carrots and asparagus. |

## Friday

| | |
|---|---|
| Breakfast | Granola with cherries and apricots. |
| Mid-morning | Soya yoghurt sprinkled with linseeds. |
| Lunch | Lentil and vegetable soup with oatcakes. |
| Dinner | Chilli bean casserole (see chapter 8). |

## Saturday

| | |
|---|---|
| Breakfast | Toast made with wheat-free or gluten-free bread. |
| Mid-morning | Soya yoghurt with linseeds. |
| Lunch | Mixed bean and brown rice salad (see chapter 8). |
| Dinner | Stuffed vegetables (see chapter 8). |

## Sunday

| | |
|---|---|
| Breakfast | Kedgeree (see chapter 8). |
| Mid-morning | Celery, peppers and baby corn with homemade hummus (see chapter 8). |
| Lunch | Sunday roast (with wheat-free gravy and Yorkshire pudding). |
| Dinner | Watercress soup with oatcakes. |

*... and drink anti-spasmodic, anti-inflammatory chamomile, peppermint or ginger tea.*

# Acne

## Monday

| | |
|---|---|
| Breakfast | Cantaloupe melon, banana and soya yoghurt smoothie. |
| Mid-morning | Snack on olives and nuts. |
| Lunch | Tomato soup and oatcakes (see chapter 8). |
| Dinner | Baked salmon steak with asparagus, carrots and sweet potato. |

## Tuesday

| | |
|---|---|
| Breakfast | Mixed fruit salad with berries, mango, apricots, peaches and red grapes sprinkled with wheat germ and mixed seeds. |
| Mid-morning | Soya yoghurt. |
| Lunch | Corn tortilla wrap with bean sprouts, cucumber, radish, onion, watercress and avocado. |
| Dinner | Brown rice and vegetable risotto. |

## Wednesday

| | |
|---|---|
| Breakfast | Granola with wheat germ, apricots, mango and mandarin segments. |
| Mid-morning | A nut or seed bar. |
| Lunch | Rocket leaves with mozzarella, tomatoes, avocado, onion, garlic, olives and pine nuts. |
| Dinner | Savoy cabbage stir-fry (see chapter 8). |

## Thursday

| | |
|---|---|
| Breakfast | Soya yoghurt with added seeds, nectarines and plums. |
| Mid-morning | Oatcakes with carrot sticks and homemade hummus (see chapter 8). |
| Lunch | Lentil soup. |
| Dinner | Seared tuna with garlic-roasted squash, carrot and broccoli. |

### Friday

| | |
|---|---|
| Breakfast | Poached egg served on a bed of spinach or seeded bread. |
| Mid-morning | Tomatoes, peppers and carrots with homemade hummus (see chapter 8). |
| Lunch | Jacket potato with tuna or hummus and a mixed salad. |
| Dinner | Superfood curry with brown rice. (See chapter 8 for recipe). |

### Saturday

| | |
|---|---|
| Breakfast | Granola mixed with cashew nuts and seeds. |
| Snacks | Olives, almonds and Brazil nuts. |
| Lunch | Mixed bean and brown rice salad (see chapter 8). |
| Dinner | Steamed fish or steak with broccoli, garlic-roasted squash and sweet potato. |

### Sunday

| | |
|---|---|
| Breakfast | Fruit salad with peaches, cantaloupe melon and berries. |
| Mid-morning | Soya yoghurt. |
| Lunch | Sunday roast. |
| Dinner | Watercress or broccoli soup |

*... and drink beta-carotene rich juices for maximum vitamin A benefits... mango, cantaloupe melon, carrot, beetroot...*

# Eczema and psoriasis

## Monday

Breakfast — Porridge with soya milk, linseeds and pumpkin seeds.

Mid-morning — Mixed fruit salad with mango, apricots, peach, red grapes and plums.

Lunch — Vegetable and lentil soup.

Dinner — Baked salmon steak with asparagus, carrots and baked sweet potato.

## Tuesday

Breakfast — Soya yoghurt with pumpkin seeds, linseeds and fruit.

Mid-morning — Asparagus, carrot and pepper sticks with homemade hummus (see chapter 8).

Lunch — Mixed bean salad with garlic, onions, watercress, radish, carrot and avocado.

Dinner — Salmon and sweet potato risotto with wilted spinach (see chapter 8).

## Wednesday

Breakfast — Granola with mixed seeds and fruit.

Mid-morning — Hummus on oatcakes with asparagus, beetroot and radish.

Lunch — Peppered mackerel with a green salad, onion, garlic, carrots, watercress and beetroot.

Dinner — Savoy cabbage stir-fry (see chapter 8).

## Thursday

Breakfast — Porridge or millet with soya, pumpkin seeds and linseeds.

Mid-morning — Fruit salad – melon, mango, red apple, red grapes, banana.

| Lunch | Brown rice Waldorf salad with raisins, walnuts, chopped apple and celery. |
| Dinner | Seared tuna steak with garlic-roasted squash, carrot and sweet potato, served with broccoli. |

## Friday

| Breakfast | Granola with mixed seeds and fruit. |
| Mid-morning | A nut or seed bar. |
| Lunch | Baked potato with hummus and a red onion and rocket salad. |
| Dinner | Chilli bean casserole with steamed brown rice (see chapter 8). |

## Saturday

| Breakfast | Soya yoghurt with seeds, cherries, mango and banana. |
| Snacks | A handful of Brazil nuts. |
| Lunch | Lentil soup with oatcakes. |
| Dinner | Steamed fish with garlic-roasted squash, sweet potato and broccoli. |

## Sunday

| Breakfast | Banana smoothie with soya yoghurt, soya milk and linseeds. |
| Mid-morning | Carrot, mange tout and baby corn with homemade hummus (see chapter 8). |
| Lunch | Sunday roast (with a wheat/gluten-free gravy mix). |
| Dinner | Watercress soup and oatcakes. |

*... and drink milk-free oolong tea or green tea.*

# Chapter Eight

# Recipes

## Mixed Bean and Brown Rice Salad

**Serves 2**

**Ingredients**
100g brown rice
1 small tin mixed beans
1 garlic clove
1 red onion
¼ of a cucumber
2-3 tomatoes
A handful of raisins
1 dessertspoon mixed seeds – pumpkin, linseed and sesame
1 tsp rapeseed, linseed or olive oil (optional)

**Method**
1. Cook the rice according to the instructions on the packet.
2. While the rice is cooking chop all the salad vegetables into small pieces and mix with the beans, seeds and raisins.
3. Mix the cooked brown rice with beans, raisins, seeds and salad.
4. Add the oil (optional).
5. Herbs or spices such as coriander, fennel or chillies may be added if desired.

# Homemade Hummus

### Ingredients
1 x 200g tin chickpeas
2 tbsp olive oil
2-3 garlic cloves, roughly chopped
Fresh lemon juice to taste

### Method
1. Place all the ingredients in a blender and blend until smooth.
2. Serve with carrot, celery, asparagus, radish, tomato, pepper…whatever crunchy, fresh vegetables you like!

# Kedgeree

### Serves 2

### Ingredients
100g brown rice
2 haddock or mackerel fillets
1 tsp turmeric
2 organic eggs, boiled
Pinch of fresh coriander

### Method
1. Cook the rice according to the instructions on the packet.
2. While the rice is cooking, poach the fish in water or skimmed milk. Use enough liquid to half cover the fish and gently simmer until the fish is cooked.
3. Mix the cooked brown rice with the fish and turmeric.
4. Chop the boiled eggs on top and add some fresh coriander.

# Tomato Soup

**Serves 2**

## Ingredients
1 tbsp olive oil
1 onion, grated
1 red chilli, de-seeded and chopped
2 garlic cloves, crushed
8 medium tomatoes, chopped
285ml vegetable stock
2 tbsp chopped parsley or basil

## Method
1. Heat the olive oil and cook the onion until soft.
2. Add the chilli and garlic and heat for another minute.
3. Add the chopped tomatoes and cook for 10 minutes.
4. Add the stock, bring to the boil and then simmer for 20 minutes (alternatively, this can be cooked in a slow cooker on low for 5-6 hours).
5. Puree the soup in a blender and serve, adding the freshly chopped parsley or basil. If you wish to, serve with pumpernickel, rye or sourdough bread.

'Any other vegetable can be used in addition to or instead of the tomatoes. Cooked lentils or beans can be added at the same time as the vegetables, but adding these as well will increase the number of portions.'

# Salmon and Sweet Potato Risotto

**Serves 2**

### Ingredients
2 salmon steaks
2 medium-sized sweet potatoes, chopped and roasted
Olive oil
2 garlic cloves, finely diced
1 onion, sliced
150g organic brown rice or risotto rice
1 bag or 4 large handfuls of rocket

### Method
1. Bake the salmon steak and roast the sweet potato in a little olive oil at 180°C/350°F/Gas Mark 4 for about 30 minutes (parboiling the sweet potato first for 10-15 minutes reduces roasting time).
2. Meanwhile, sauté some garlic and onion in a pan with a little olive oil.
3. Add the rice, stirring to coat it with the oil, onion and garlic mixture.
4. Add enough water to cover the rice and allow to simmer, adding extra water as required until the rice is cooked. If you parboiled the sweet potato, use the water from this.
5. Once the rice is cooked, add the roasted sweet potato, rocket and baked salmon (broken into chunks) and serve.

# Savoy Cabbage Stir-Fry

**Serves 2**

## Ingredients
2 tsp olive oil
1 onion, chopped
2 garlic cloves, sliced
1 savoy cabbage
A handful of mushrooms
A handful of frozen peas
A handful of sweetcorn or baby corn
A handful of mange tout
A handful of peppers
1 portion of tofu, chicken or turkey
½ tin baked beans or tinned tomatoes

## Method
1. Heat a little olive oil in a pan.
2. Add the chopped onion and the cloves of sliced garlic.
3. Any herbs or spices can also be added at this time (such as chopped chilli, turmeric, oregano or ginger).
4. Cut the savoy cabbage into thin strips and add to the pan.
5. Once the onion and cabbage are slightly browned, add the other vegetables.
6. Add a portion of tofu, chicken or turkey and stir until cooked through.
7. Add half a tin of baked beans or tinned tomatoes to create a sauce. Stir until heated through and serve with brown rice or rice noodles.

# Chilli Bean Casserole

**Serves 2-4**

**Ingredients**
2 tsp olive oil
1 onion, chopped
2 garlic cloves, chopped
1-2 chillies, chopped
A handful of mushrooms
2 carrots, diced
A handful of frozen peas and sweetcorn
A handful of fresh/frozen peppers
Tin of tomatoes
Tin of mixed beans
150g brown rice

**Method**
1. Brown the onion and garlic in a little olive oil and then add the fresh chillies.
2. Add the mushrooms, carrots, peas and peppers to the pan along with the tinned tomatoes and mixed beans.
3. Simmer for 30 minutes.
4. Serve with brown rice.

# Superfood Curry

**Serves 2**

## Ingredients
1 tsp olive oil
2 garlic cloves, chopped
1 onion, chopped
Handful of fresh coriander
2 tsp turmeric
2 red chillies, chopped
2 carrots, diced
1 large sweet potato, diced
3 large fresh tomatoes, chopped
1 vegetable stock cube made into 300ml
1 small tin chickpeas
1 head of broccoli
1 small pot fat-free Greek yoghurt
150g brown rice

## Method
1. Heat the oil and cook the garlic and onion until soft.
2. Add a tsp of finely chopped coriander, the turmeric and the chillies. Stir and cook for two minutes.
3. Add the carrots, sweet potato and tomatoes.
4. Add the liquid stock and chickpeas, bring to the boil and then simmer for approximately 20 minutes.
5. Meanwhile, blanch the broccoli and add once the curry is cooked.
6. Remove from the heat. Allow to cool slightly before adding the yoghurt.
7. Sprinkle a generous helping of fresh coriander on top and serve with brown rice.

# Stuffed Vegetables

**Serves 2**

**Ingredients**

2 medium baked potatoes with skin
1 tsp olive oil
2 garlic cloves, chopped
1 onion, chopped
A handful of mushrooms
1 dessertspoon of mixed seeds – pumpkin, sunflower and sesame seeds
A handful of peas
A handful of fresh or frozen sweetcorn
100g fresh spinach
2 large peppers, raw, with tops cut off
Green salad

**Method**

1. Bake the potatoes until cooked.
2. Meanwhile, heat a little oil and lightly stir-fry the garlic, onion and mushrooms.
3. Add the seeds, peas and sweetcorn and heat through, adding the spinach.
4. Stir until the spinach has wilted and remove from the heat.
5. Cut the top off the potatoes and scoop out the mash into the stir-fry and mix.
6. Once thoroughly mixed, stuff the peppers and potatoes with the mixture and bake for 35 minutes at 180°C/356°F/Gas Mark 4.
7. Serve with a large green salad.

Need2Know

# Seared Tuna Steak with Roasted Root Vegetables

**Serves 2**

**Ingredients**

2 root vegetables (choose from a large squash, a large sweet potato or two carrots)
1 tsp olive oil
2 tuna steaks
1 large head of broccoli
4 garlic cloves

**Method**

1. Chop the vegetables into chunks and parboil in boiling water for 10-15 minutes.
2. Meanwhile, heat the olive oil in a baking tray in the oven at 180°C/356°F/ Gas Mark 4.
3. Peel the garlic cloves and crush slightly.
4. Sieve the vegetables and add carefully to the hot oil with the garlic to roast for approximately 40 minutes.
5. Approximately 20 minutes before the vegetables are ready, steam or lightly boil the broccoli.
6. Lightly oil a pan and add the tuna steaks; sear them on each side at a medium to high temperature.

'Try swapping tuna steak for swordfish or marlin steaks in this recipe.'

# Help List

## Finding a practitioner to help

### British Association for Applied Nutrition and Nutritional Therapy (BANT)

www.bant.org.uk
BANT is a professional body for nutritional therapists and those working in the field of nutritional science. A list of nutritional registered practitioners can be found on the BANT website, along with information explaining the differences between dietitians, nutritionists and nutritional therapists.

### British Nutrition Foundation

www.nutrition.org.uk
The British Nutrition Foundation is a credible source of nutrition information. It provides reliable information on food, nutrition and healthy eating, as well as topical news items and scientific research.

### Dietitians Unlimited

www.dietitiansunlimited.co.uk
A website which can help you to find a private or freelance dietician in the UK.

## Nutrition and cooking

### 5 A DAY

www.5aday.nhs.uk
NHS website with lots of information about healthy eating laid out in an easy-to-understand format, with video clips, wall charts and simple tips to help you follow a healthier diet.

## Change4Life

www.nhs.uk/change4life

Change4Life is a government campaign aimed at getting people fit and healthy. Although the campaign is being run throughout England only, the website still contains lots of useful information and tips aimed at getting people more active and improving eating habits.

## Department of Health

www.dh.gov.uk

This website provides information on national healthy eating initiatives such as '5 A DAY' and 'Change4Life'.

## Eatwell

www.eatwell.gov.uk

This is a more 'light weight' reader-friendly website of the Food Standards Agency which is a little more geared towards the general public. The eatwell website provides a wealth of trustworthy, practical information about food and healthy eating such as tips on what to eat for a healthy heart, how to help prevent osteoporosis and which foods may boost mental function.

## Food Standards Agency

Aviation House, 125 Kingsway, London, WC2B 6NH
Tel: 0207 276 8829
www.food.gov.uk

**Scotland**
6th Floor, St Magnus House, 25 Guild Street, Aberdeen, AB11 6NJ
Tel: 01224 285100

**Northern Ireland**
10 A-C Clarendon Road, Belfast, BT1 3BG
Tel: 02890 417700

**Wales**
11th Floor, South Gate House, Wood Street, Cardiff, CF10 1EW
Tel: 02920 678999

The Food Standards Agency is an independent government department which provides factual nutrition information, providing a reliable and credible source of nutrition information for consumers. The website offers a wide range of reports, nutrition information sheets, recipes and healthy eating tips.

## Patrick Holford

www.patrickholford.com
Leading nutritionist's website packed with information and advice about healthy eating.

# Healthy hearts

## Blood Pressure Association

www.bpassoc.org.uk
A UK-wide charity aiming to lower the nation's blood pressure by providing information, support and awareness raising activities.

## British Heart Foundation

www.bhf.org.uk
The British Heart Foundation provide information and research on cardiovascular disease. Their website contains information on keeping your heart healthy and living with a heart condition.

## British Hypertension Society

www.bhsoc.org
Provides a medical and scientific research forum to understand blood pressure and improve its treatment.

## High Blood Pressure Foundation

www.hbpf.org.uk
A charity dedicated to improving understanding, assessment, treatment and public awareness of high blood pressure.

# Healthy bones

## Arthritis Care

www.arthritiscare.org.uk
Arthritis Care is the UK's largest charity organisation for people with arthritis. The website provides information on arthritis, events and news.

## Arthritis Research UK

www.arthritisresearchuk.org
Charity leading the fight against arthritis.

## National Osteoporosis Society

www.nos.org.uk
The National Osteoporosis Society is the only UK-wide charity dedicated to improving the diagnosis, prevention and treatment of osteoporosis.

# Diabetes

## Diabetes UK

www.diabetes.org.uk
Diabetes UK is the largest organisation in the UK working for people with diabetes, funding research, campaigning and helping people live with the condition.

# Healthy minds

## Alzheimer's Research Trust

www.alzheimers-research.org.uk
The Alzheimer's Research Trust describes itself as the 'UK's leading research charity for dementia'. As well as funding research, it provides information on Alzheimer's and current research.

# Alzheimer's Society

www.alzheimers.org.uk
The Alzheimer's Society aims to improve the quality of life for people affected by Alzheimer's.

# British Dyslexia Association

www.bdadyslexia.org.uk
Helps with early ID and support in schools for dyslexic pupils and school leavers in higher education and the workplace. Aims to influence the government and other institutions.

# Dementia UK

www.dementiauk.org
Charity working to improve quality of life for all people affected by dementia.

# Food and Behaviour Research

www.fabresearch.org
A great website for information, factsheets and research on conditions where behaviour, learning and mood are linked with food and nutrition.

# Mental Health Foundation

www.mentalhealth.org.uk
This website offers information and downloadable information leaflets on a range of mental health conditions as well as podcasts for general wellbeing and latest news to relevant conditions.

# Mind (National Association for Mental Health)

www.mind.org.uk
Provides services throughout England and Wales for people with mental health problems, and campaigns for better treatment, patients' rights and better medical practices.

### National Association for Premenstrual Syndrome

www.pms.org.uk
National Association for Premenstrual Syndrome is the leading membership organisation supporting people affected by PMS.

### National Autistic Society

www.autism.org.uk
Leading UK charity with branches in Scotland, Northern Ireland, Wales and England.

# Healthy tums

### Coeliac UK

www.coeliac.org.uk
The national organisation for people with coeliac disease, providing information about the condition, symptoms and diagnosis.

### CORE

www.corecharity.org.uk
This is the only UK charity that funds research into gut, liver, intestinal and bowel illnesses. It aims to provide the public with clear facts and information about these conditions. See their website for case studies, research and information about fundraising events.

### The Gut Trust

www.theguttrust.org
The Gut Trust is the UK's charity for IBS. Their website is packed with useful information and helpful advice for parents, children and teenagers.

### IBS Research Appeal

www.ibsresearchupdate.org
An IBS charity based at Central Middlesex Hospital in London which funds a research programme into the causes and treatments of IBS, directed by gastroenterologist Professor David Silk, MD, FRCP.

# Healthy skin

## British Association of Dermatologists

www.bad.org.uk

BAD preserves books relating to the history of dermatology. It also organises an annual conference and has commissioned a regional history of dermatology. It is a professional organisation for all dermatologists in the UK. They aim to support patients and improve practice standards. The website includes general information on skin, dermatology and various skin diseases.

## National Eczema Society

www.eczema.org

National Eczema Society provides people with independent and practical advice about treating and managing eczema.

## The Psoriasis Association

www.psoriasis-association.org.uk

The Psoriasis Association is the leading national membership organisation for people affected by psoriasis – patients, families, carers and health professionals.

## Skin Care Campaign

www.skincarecampaign.org

The Skin Care Campaign is a subsidiary of the National Eczema Society, representing the interests of people in the UK with skin diseases.

# Book List

**Acid and Alkaline**
By Herman Aihara, George Ohsawa Macrobiotic Foundation, USA, 1986.

**Acne – The Essential Guide**
By Antonia Mariconda, Need2Know, Peterborough, 2009.

**ADHD – The Essential Guide**
By Diane Paul, Need2Know, Peterborough, 2008.

**Alzheimer's – The Essential Guide**
By Jackie Cosh, Need2Know, Peterborough, 2009.

**Autism – A Parent's Guide**
By Hilary Hawkes, Need2Know, Peterborough, 2009.

**Blood Pressure – The Essential Guide**
By Dr Justine Davies, Need2Know, Peterborough, 2009.

**Coeliac Disease – The Essential Guide**
By Kate Coxon, Need2Know, Peterborough, 2010.

**Diabetes – The Essential Guide**
By Sue Marshall, Need2Know, Peterborough, 2008.

**Dyslexia – A Parent's Guide**
By Maria Chivers, Need2Know, Peterborough, 2009.

**Encyclopedia of Natural Medicine**
By Michael Murray and Joseph Pizzorno, Three Rivers Press, USA, 1998.

**Foods That Harm, Foods That Heal**
By Readers Digest, Readers Digest Association, London, 2004.

**GI How To Succeed Using A Glycaemic Index Diet**
By Harper Collins, HarperCollins Publishers, Glasgow, 2005.

**Irritable Bowel Syndrome – The Essential Guide**
By Sarah Dawson, Need2Know, Peterborough, 2009.

**Lose Weight, Gain Energy, Get Healthy**
By Sara Kirkham, Hodder, London, 2010.

**The Mediterranean Diet**
By Marissa Cloutier and Eve Adamson, HarperCollins, Glasgow, 2004.

**The Optimum Nutrition Bible**
By Patrick Holford, Piatkus, London, 1997.

**Vitamin D: Physiology, Molecular Biology and Clinical Applications**
By Michael F Holick, Humana Press, USA, 1998.

**Weight Loss – The Essential Guide**
By Sara Kirkham, Need2Know, Peterborough, 2010.

**What Colour Is Your Diet?**
By David Heber, HarperCollins, Glasgow, 2001.

# References

Ameye LG and Chee WS, 'Osteoarthritis and nutrition. From nutraceuticals to functional foods: a systematic review of the scientific evidence', *Arthritis Research and Therapy*, 2008, vol. 8, pages 1-22, www.ncbi.nlm.nih.gov/pubmed/16859534, accessed 19 July 2010.

Buckley D, Muench J and Hamilton A, 'How effective are dietary interventions in lowering lipids in adults with dyslipidemia?', *The Journal of Family Practice*, 2007, vol. 56, pages 46-8, www.jfponline.com/Pages.asp?AID=4688&issue=January%202007&UID, accessed 19 July 2010.

Buscemi S *et al.,* 'Acute effects of coffee on endothelial function in healthy subjects', *European Journal of Clinical Nutrition,* 2010, vol. 64, pages 483-9, www.ncbi.nlm.nih.gov/pubmed/20125186, accessed 19 July 2010.

Dai Q *et al.,* 'Fruit and Vegetable Juices and Alzheimer's Disease: The Kame Project', *The American Journal of Medicine*, 2006, vol. 119, pages 751-9, www.ncbi.nlm.nih.gov/pmc/articles/PMC2266591/pdf/nihms37963.pdf, accessed 29 July 2010.

Diabetes UK, *What is Diabetes?*, www.diabetes.org.uk/Guide-to-diabetes/Introduction-to-diabetes/What_is_diabetes/, accessed 29 July 2010.

Food Standards Agency, *McCance and Widdowson's The Composition of Foods* (6th edition), The Food Standards Agency, London, 2002.

*The Food Magazine*, The Food Commission (UK) Ltd, London, 2007, www.foodmagazine.org.uk.

Karatay S *et al.,* 'The effect of individualized diet challenges consisting of allergenic foods on TNF-alpha and IL-1beta levels in patients with rheumatoid arthritis', *Rheumatology,* 2004, vol. 43, pages 429-33, http://rheumatology.oxfordjournals.org/cgi/reprint/43/11/1429, accessed 19 July 2010.

Lee KW *et al.,* 'Cocoa has more phenolic phytochemicals and a higher antioxidant capacity than teas and red wine', *Journal of Agriculture and Food Chemistry,* 2003, vol 51, pages 7292-5. Abstract available at http://www.ncbi.nlm.nih.gov/pubmed/14640573, accessed 8 Oct 2010.

Marcellini *et al.,* 'Psychosocial Aspects and Zinc Status: Is There a Relationship with Successful Aging?', *Rejuvenation Research*, 2009, vol. 9, pages 333-37.

Mineharu Y *et al.,* 'Coffee, green tea, black tea and oolong tea consumption and risk of mortality from cardiovascular disease in Japanese men and women', *Journal of Epidemiology and Community Health*, December 2009.

NHS, *One in four affected*, 2010, www.nhs.uk/Livewell/mentalhealth/Pages/Mentalhealthoverview.aspx, accessed 29 July 2010.

Sawitzke AD *et al.,* 'The effect of glucosamine and/or chondroitin sulfate on the progression of knee osteoarthritis: a report from the glucosamine/chondroitin arthritis intervention trial', *Arthritis and Rheumatism*, 2008, vol 58, pages 3183-91.

Sobenin, I A *et al.,* 'Time-released garlic powder tablets lower systolic and diastolic blood pressure in men with mild and moderate arterial hypertension', *Hypertension Research*, 2009, vol. 32, pages 433-7.

Uehara M *et al.,* 'A trial of oolong tea in the management of recalcitrant atopic dermatitis', *Archives of Dermatology*, 2001, vol. 137, pages 42-3, http://archderm.ama-assn.org/cgi/reprint/137/1/42, accessed 29 July 2010.

The Vegetarian Society, 'Omega 3 fats', http://www.vegsoc.org/info/omega3.html, accessed 8 October 2010.

World Health Organisation, *Cardiovascular disease: prevention and control*, 2003, www.who.int/dietphysicalactivity/publications/facts/cvd/en/, accessed 29 July 2010.

# Glossary

**Allergen**

A substance that prompts an allergic reaction or intolerance in the body.

**Anthocyanidins**

A group of nutrients found in abundance in dark red or purple fruits and vegetables such as red grapes, cherries and berries containing compounds with therapeutic antioxidant properties.

**Antioxidant**

Compounds or nutrients with antioxidant properties that counteract free radical oxidation in the body. Examples include beta carotene, vitamins C and E, zinc and selenium.

**Carotenoids**

A group of nutrients with therapeutic and antioxidant properties found predominantly in orange coloured fruits and vegetables such as apricots, mango, carrots and sweet potato. Also found in beetroot and dark green leafy vegetables.

**Catechins**

Catechins are health-promoting food compounds with antioxidant and anti-inflammatory properties. They are found in grape seeds and green tea.

**Docosahexanoic acid**

Docosahexanoic acid (DHA), a long-chain fatty acid found in fish.

**Eicosapentaenoic acid**

Eicosapentaenoic acid (EHA), a long-chain fatty acid found in fish.

**Fatty acid**

Fats in food are formed from triglycerides, which are formed from a molecule of glycerol and three fatty acids. Each fatty acid is either saturated, monounsaturated or polyunsaturated, depending upon the number of hydrogen atoms and degree of saturation. Fatty acids such as omega 3 or omega 6 fatty acids have various therapeutic roles in the body.

### Flavonoids

A group of compounds with anti-allergic, anti-bacterial, antioxidant and anti-inflammatory properties. Anthocyanidins, isoflavonoids and catechins are all types of flavonoid, commonly found in onions, apples, red wine and tea.

### Fructose

A type of monosaccharide sugar found in fruit.

### Galactose

A monosaccharide sugar that makes lactose (milk sugar) together with glucose.

### Glucose

The main monosaccharide sugar found in food. Used in the human body as a major source of fuel.

### Glycaemic index

The glycaemic index (GI) is a measure of how quickly the glucose in foods is absorbed into the bloodstream – a low GI will mean the food has low glucose content or contains mostly slow release starches. A high-GI score indicates a food provides energy more quickly.

### Glycaemic load

The glycaemic load of a food relates to the effect that a normal portion of food or drink will have on blood sugar levels. It depends on the GI of the carbohydrate and also how much carbohydrate a typical portion contains. It can be calculated as follows:

$$\frac{\text{glycaemic index (GI) x the weight (g) of carbohydrate to be eaten}}{100}$$

### HDL cholesterol

This 'good' type of cholesterol formed with high density lipoproteins (HDL) carries cholesterol back to the liver, reducing blood cholesterol levels and aiding cholesterol removal via the liver and gall bladder out of the body.

### Hydrogenated fat

A type of processed fat that originated as a liquid polyunsaturated fat, but has become saturated after being passed through hydrogen so that hydrogen atoms attach to the fatty acid and create a synthetic saturated fat.

## Inulin

A type of plant fibre that is useful for reducing cholesterol absorption in the digestive tract. Found in chicory, Jerusalem artichokes, garlic, onion and asparagus.

## LDL cholesterol

Low density lipoprotein (LDL) is known as 'bad' cholesterol as it is this type of cholesterol that becomes oxidised and can contribute to atherosclerosis, the 'furring' of the arteries.

## Monosaccharide

Monosaccharides are the building blocks of carbohydrate foods. When carbohydrates are digested, they are eventually broken down into these single sugars. The most common type is glucose.

## Monounsaturated fat

A type of fatty acid with one double bond in its structure, typically found in high amounts in olives, olive oil and avocados. Because there is only one double bond in these fatty acids, they limit oxidation (when oxygen atoms connect to a fatty acid) when heated, reducing the risk of oxidation of fats and free radical oxidation in the body.

## *Oxalates*

Foods such as spinach and rhubarb are rich in these compounds, where oxalic acid is bound to calcium. The calcium in calcium oxalate is poorly absorbed into the body via the digestive system.

## Oxalic acid

Oxalic acid connects to calcium in foods to form calcium oxalate, a form of calcium poorly absorbed into the body.

## Oxidation

There are several different chemical reactions which cause oxidation, but in the context of this book, oxidation is referring to unstable atoms or molecules attaching to neighbouring molecules or cells and destabilising them. This can result in a chain reaction of molecular damage causing cell damage. Heated and processed fats (trans and hydrogenated fats) are most likely to become oxidised.

## Phytates

Phytates are found in bran and the outside of wholegrains. They can bind to calcium in the digestive system and hinder its absorption into the body.

### Phytic acid

Phytic acid connects to calcium in foods to form calcium phytate, a form of calcium poorly absorbed into the body.

### Phytoestrogen

A plant form of the hormone oestrogen which is also capable of having oestrogenic effects on body cells.

### Phytosterol

Plant derivative of cholesterol which competes for absorption with the animal sterol cholesterol, thereby reducing cholesterol absorption into the body. Phytosterols are commonly found in plant oils. They are often added to margarines and yoghurts in order to reduce cholesterol levels.

### Plaque

A build up of oxidised cholesterol, fats and white blood cells found on the inside of arteries causing the condition known as atherosclerosis. This build up of deposits within the arteries reduces the artery diameter, leaving less space for blood to pass through, thereby increasing blood pressure.

### Polyphenol

A group of nutrients (found in abundance in dark red or purple fruits and vegetables such as red grapes, cherries and berries) containing compounds with therapeutic antioxidant properties.

### Polysaccharide

A chain of monosaccharide sugars joined together to form a chain. Some polysaccharides form digestible starch in the diet, others form non-digestable compounds known as fibre.

### Polyunsaturated fat

A type of fatty acid with more than one double bond in the structure typically found in high amounts in fish, nuts, seeds and oils such as safflower or sunflower oil. The number of double bonds in these unsaturated fatty acids make them liable to oxidation when heated which is why monounsaturated oils are deemed more healthy to cook with.

### Refined fat

A type of fat that has been highly processed, such as hydrogenated, partially hydrogenated and trans fats.

## Saturated fat
A type of fatty acid with no double bond in the structure typically found in meats and dairy produce, and also some vegetable foods such as coconut. The complete molecular saturation makes these fats less liable to oxidation but saturated fats contribute to elevated cholesterol and heart disease.

## Serotonin
A type of neurotransmitter known as the 'feel good' hormone, as it induces feelings of wellbeing, relaxation and initiates sleep.

## Stanols and sterols
Plant stanols and sterols are natural plant nutrients added to foods such as margarines, yoghurts and soft cheeses to reduce cholesterol.

## Trans fat
A type of chemically altered fat formed during hydrogenation. The term 'trans' refers to the arrangement of atoms around the double bond(s); the structure of a trans fat aids saturation due to 'gaps' in its structure where hydrogen atoms can attach, and prevents enzymes or other substances attaching to the fatty acid, denaturing its natural functions.

## Triglyceride
The basic structure of fats is the triglyceride, formed from a molecule of glycerol and three fatty acid chains.

## Tryptophan
An essential amino acid required by the human body. It is used to form various protein molecules, including the neurotransmitter serotonin.

# Need - 2 - Know

**Need −2− Know**

## Available Titles Include ...

**Allergies** A Parent's Guide
ISBN 978-1-86144-064-8 £8.99

**Autism** A Parent's Guide
ISBN 978-1-86144-069-3 £8.99

**Drugs** A Parent's Guide
ISBN 978-1-86144-043-3 £8.99

**Dyslexia and Other Learning Difficulties**
A Parent's Guide   ISBN 978-1-86144-042-6 £8.99

**Bullying** A Parent's Guide
ISBN 978-1-86144-044-0 £8.99

**Epilepsy** The Essential Guide
ISBN 978-1-86144-063-1 £8.99

**Teenage Pregnancy** The Essential Guide
ISBN 978-1-86144-046-4 £8.99

**Gap Years** The Essential Guide
ISBN 978-1-86144-079-2 £8.99

**How to Pass Exams** A Parent's Guide
ISBN 978-1-86144-047-1 £8.99

**Child Obesity** A Parent's Guide
ISBN 978-1-86144-049-5 £8.99

**Applying to University** The Essential Guide
ISBN 978-1-86144-052-5 £8.99

**ADHD** The Essential Guide
ISBN 978-1-86144-060-0 £8.99

**Student Cookbook - Healthy Eating** The Essential Guide
ISBN 978-1-86144-061-7 £8.99

**Stress** The Essential Guide
ISBN 978-1-86144-054-9 £8.99

**Adoption and Fostering** A Parent's Guide
ISBN 978-1-86144-056-3 £8.99

**Special Educational Needs** A Parent's Guide
ISBN 978-1-86144-057-0 £8.99

**The Pill** An Essential Guide
ISBN 978-1-86144-058-7 £8.99

**University** A Survival Guide
ISBN 978-1-86144-072-3 £8.99

**Diabetes** The Essential Guide
ISBN 978-1-86144-059-4 £8.99

View the full range at **www.need2knowbooks.co.uk**. To order our titles, call **01733 898103**, email **sales@n2kbooks.com** or visit the website.

**Need - 2 - Know**, Remus House, Coltsfoot Drive, Peterborough, PE2 9JX